Scriptless

What I Learned About God on the Las Vegas Strip

Andrea Coli

This book is unreservedly dedicated to Chris. Without your support and inspiration this book would still just be rolling around in my head...and actually, not even that, since you were the one who encouraged me to pursue improvisation in the first place. You're one of the best decisions I ever made.

Acknowledgements

Thank you to Liz Allen, director extraordinaire, improvisation mentor, and friend. It is always a blast to dialogue with you (about any topic really, but especially improvisation). I am truly grateful for your insights, gentle critiques and encouragement regarding this book. Thank you for graciously letting me steal so much of your wisdom!

To my cast mates at The Second City: Gretchen Baker, Don Bowsher, Michael Hartnett, Damian Mace, Shannon MacIntyre, Homer Marrs, Paul Mattingly, Veronica Moorhead, Darren Pitura, Derek Shipman, Jeynifer Tribbitt, Marcus Weiss, and Joshua Zehner. Thank you for teaching me what ensemble really means.

I want to thank my producer Brooke Shoening, for seeing some potential in me and giving me a spot in The Second City Scriptless; Jen Porter and Shatha Farij for being more than just great stage managers. Thanks to the crew Edwin Horton, Dave Weinberg and Bill Rudolph.

I want to thank my editor Beth Deese. I am so appreciative of your grammar smarts (that's probably not grammatically correct) and your insight about the content of each chapter. Thank you for supporting the whole concept and walking me through my first book. Tasha Buser, your thoughtful read-throughs meant more to me than you can know. Thank you for taking my writing to heart. Ben Parker, thank you for reading my mind and creating a cover that is exactly what I wanted. Kristina Rogers, thank you for using your time and talent to take an exceptional cover photo.

Thanks to my mom and dad and step-parents for encouraging my humor and supporting me in everything I do. Thanks also to Jim and Karen for seeing and loving me like a real daughter. Chris, you have been a cheerleader and coach in this whole process. Thank you for the myriad of conversations about each and every chapter of this book.

Contents

Chapter 1
Make It Up on the Spot

I've always been the goofy kid. I don't necessarily mean goofy looking, although from about 1983 to 1989 that was also true. By goofy I mean silly and fun-loving. As far back as I can remember I was good at making people laugh. I'd say funny stuff or make weird faces. Sometimes I'd talk to my friends in strange accents or just act like a dork to get a laugh. Little did I know that because of these traits I would find my way to a Las Vegas comedy stage, and my experience there would turn into a book about my relationship with God. But I'm getting ahead of myself. Let's back up. It all started with two phone calls, four years apart...

The first was in the early spring of 2000, just a few months after my husband Chris and I had moved to Michigan. I grew up in Southern California and had never lived anywhere else for the first 25 years of my life. If I had orchestrated the timing of the move, I would have planned for late summer. I would have enjoyed the trees in their fullness, then welcomed the beautiful fall colors and transitioned seamlessly into the cold of winter. But, no, we moved on December 1st. I was thinking, "It's bitterly cold. None of my socks are thick enough. What does wind chill mean? Seven is not a temperature, it's the age of a small child! Why can't I feel my nose?"

The transition to life in Michigan was abrupt. I wasn't sure what this new life would look like, but what I soon learned was that there was something there called The Second City, and it was about to make a big impact on me.

Chris grew up outside of Chicago, which is the home of The Second City, the hub of sketch comedy and improvisation. I'd never heard of it, but he told me that I'd heard of many of its alumni. People like Bill Murray, Dan Aykroyd, Shelley Long, Mike Meyers, Chris Farley, Steve Carell, Stephen Colbert, Tina Fey and Amy Poehler just to name a few. These people had worked their way up the ranks to Saturday Night Live and similar shows by way of their experience at The Second City. For years I had been involved in the drama ministry at our church and had some speaking experience but had never really done any improvisation. Chris encouraged me to check out the classes that The Second City Detroit was offering, so that's what I did. I guess I thought if nothing else it will help me improve my "up-front" skills that I used at church.

Getting into The Second City's Training Conservatory required an audition. The first call, the one I got in early spring of 2000, was from The Second City Detroit telling me that they liked my audition and that I was "in." I couldn't believe it. I wanted to tell everyone around me, but the problem was that at the time I worked in an assisted living facility. And as hard as they tried, those octogenarians just couldn't fully appreciate why I wanted to do a "play" with no "script." So we just went back to playing Bingo.

I started classes a few weeks later, and it was a total blast! Throughout the next couple of years I completed six levels of training at the Conservatory, and thoroughly enjoyed this new world I had discovered. Eventually, though, I felt that I had gone as far as I could go. I had gotten what I wanted out of it and I assumed that was it for me when it came to improvisation. So I closed that chapter of my life.

In late 2003, Chris and I moved again to Las Vegas, along with our then three-month-old daughter Quinn. I guess we were looking to thaw out from our time in Michigan! Actually, we relocated because Chris is a pastor, and he had accepted a position in Vegas.

A few months after the move, I found out from a friend in Michigan that The Second City had a location in Las Vegas as well, and they were holding auditions for a new show. It was an all-improvised show (kind of like "Whose Line Is It Anyway?") that would run in tandem with their regular sketch comedy show on the Strip. My thought process went something like this:

> *Hey that's interesting. And it's not like I'm real busy or anything. I'm getting a little bored with the baby conversations I'm having all day. What would it be like to interact with actual adults? Plus, I could make a little money. Oh, who am I kidding? It would be a long shot to say the least. At the same time, what do I have to lose? No*

one even knows me here. When they reject me outright at least I can say I tried and then get back to my exciting life of midnight feedings, spit up and dirty diapers. OK, so tell me more about this audition.

My second call came a few days after the audition inviting me to be in the first cast of "The Second City Scriptless."

Improvisation is all about making stuff up on the spot based on suggestions from the audience. Scriptless consisted of a bunch of scenes, improvisational games and even songs that we made up as we went along. None of it was scripted. It was pure improvisation. Although I had studied improvisation, I quickly realized that I still had a lot to learn about the craft. Lucky for me they hired a director for our show to coach us through the process. Her name is Liz Allen.

Liz is one of those people whose head and heart are equal partners in the art of improvisation. What I mean is that, mentally she is well-versed, very capable and super smart. So as a director she is very intentional about teaching the tools of good improvisation. At the same time, she is extremely intuitive and fully invests her emotions and instincts into her coaching, which taught us a lot about doing the same, a necessity for improvisation as you can imagine. But what I think she is best at is stripping away the fluff to expose the pure, unadulterated rules of great improvisation. Under her direction we grew as a cast. We became more focused, intentional and connected.

So you might be wondering, "If you are just making it up, why are there rules? Isn't that the opposite of just making it up?" Well, you're not wrong, but here's the deal. Usually when we think of rules we think of hard and fast, must-be-this-way non-negotiables. Rules establish what we are supposed to do or what we are not allowed to do. Rules in improvisation, on the other hand, aren't so much guidelines about what you can or can't do. But they are guidelines for what you should or shouldn't do if you want to create compelling scenes.

Like any skill in life, while there may be many ways to make something work, there are usually standard practices that are tried and true methods of success. In this book, I'll share some of those ideas, such as: say yes, don't ask questions, turn off your filter, and be in the moment.

As I said, even though I was performing in the show on the Strip, I still had a lot to learn about the rules. So, I really embraced what Liz was teaching us, and in the midst of it, something unexpected happened. While my improvisation skills grew, what also started to grow in me was the realization that what I was learning about the stage had striking parallels to my faith.

At every turn it seemed the experience I was having in Scriptless was teaching me about God. I began to realize that the "rules" of improvisation, if applied on a spiritual level, were offering me new insight about what my relationship with God could, and even should, look like. That is what this book is all about. Each chapter explains a principle of improvisation or tells a story of something that happened in our show as a metaphor for living out a personal faith in Christ.

I've written this book with believers in mind, but if you don't consider yourself a Christian let me first say thanks for taking the time to read this book. If you approach it with an open heart, I know that there will be something for you here. And if it intrigues you enough to consider what a relationship with God might look like for you, then every hour

I've spent on this book will have been well worth it. I truly appreciate you letting me be a small part of your spiritual journey.

And if you are a Christian, my hope is that as you read what follows you will be inspired to a greater level of faith and a stronger connection to God. My purpose is to offer a unique perspective that might breathe new life into your relationship with God, no matter where you are in that walk.

And finally, please know that more than anything, I'm just trying to figure this all out myself. The ideas here are sort of a record of the process that is going on in me. So, you may find yourself discovering different applications or nuances to the truths I'm presenting. If that happens, I will count it as the Holy Spirit speaking His words to you through something that I happen to write. It would be just like Him to do that.

So let's explore together how improvisation can be a metaphor for a relationship with God. (This is the part where you say "Yes" and we move to chapter two, which is appropriately titled "Say Yes.")

Chapter 2
Say "Yes"

When you're making up a scene on the spot, (which is what you are doing when you improvise) you must always "say yes." You say "yes" to your scene partner no matter what. If they declare that you are the Queen of Egypt, then yes...you are the Queen of Egypt. If they complain that you are lost in the woods, then yes...you are lost in the woods. If they say that your arm just fell off due to a nasty case of gangrene, then guess what? You got it.

It's up to each person to contribute to the scene and move it forward. (We'll talk about that in the next chapter.) Saying "yes" means that when someone adds an element to the scene everyone else accepts what they have said as truth. They "say yes" to the contribution. In saying "yes" you show that you buy in to the reality that has been established in the scene, and it allows your audience to do the same.

Liz, our director, would constantly be telling us to say "yes" throughout the whole show. She wanted it to become second nature to us. She worked this into us until we said "yes" at every opportunity. Sometimes, as a sort of test, she would count how many times in our one hour show we would actually use the word then that would be the only criterion for whether is was a successful show or not.

At the end of the show, regardless of how we felt the performance went, if the number of times we said the word "yes" was too low, she would tell us we still had a lot of work to do. And, conversely, if the show felt only so-so to us, but we said "yes" like there's no tomorrow, then she would tell us that it was successful in her eyes. It seems like a very black and white way to evaluate, but here's why she did it. She knew that if we could outwardly say "yes" again and again, it would eventually seep its way into our thought process. She wanted us to be thinking "yes" because on stage, what you believe inside plays out in how you respond to your fellow performers. If we verbally affirmed one another's ideas, then actually accepting each other's ideas would come naturally.

And that's exactly what happened. After a few months of intense focus on just saying "yes," we became a totally different group. There was an openness and vulnerability because we knew we would be accepted by each other. Ultimately it transformed us into a stronger cast. We had an unshakeable foundation that could support any scene in which we found ourselves. Having a strong foundation in saying "yes" is huge in improvisation. Since you don't know what you are ultimately building at least you can be secure knowing there is a solid foundation. When everyone on the stage has an openness to and acceptance of each other, you know that no matter where the scene ends up you will be there together.

Here's an example of a scene that builds on the foundation of "yes":

"I saw the sign outside about dance lessons."

"Yep. You're in the right place."

"Wait a minute. It's you!"

"Most women do recognize me."

21

(Now remember, these two actors don't know any more about this scene that you do. They are making it up as they go and supporting each other through saying "yes.")

"Recognize you? You're like my idol!"

"I'm flattered."

"It's not every day you meet the world's foremost Lambada dance expert!"

"Well I meet him everyday...in the mirror."

"Sergio Esparto! Teach me! Teach me everything you know."

"You have come to me at the right time. I have been looking for a protégé to take over my place in the world of Lambada dancing. You are that woman!"

"I'm going to faint. It's a dream come true!"

Now the foundation is laid, and we have somewhere for the scene to go. My guess is that it will involve a lot of unnecessary hip gyration on Sergio's part. The beauty of it is that the characters in the scene didn't know where their "yes" would take them, but they gave it unreservedly because that is what you must do when you improvise. If "yes" had not been given the world would have missed out on the Brazilian dance stylings of the one and only Sergio Esparto. And that would have been a real shame.

Certainly there are lots of improvised scenes less ridiculous than that one. In some scenes, "yes" allows you to return home after a fight, it enables you to face a crisis, it gets you to admit you are in love. "Yes" opens the door to any possibility. And once the door is open the potential is limitless.

That is the power of "yes."

When I think of how this works with God and me, I realize that there, too, "yes" is imperative. Like a scene partner, He puts His ideas out there and is waiting to see if I accept what He has to offer. It's as if He is trying to establish some new realities for me, and I have the choice of whether or not to say "yes" to them.

It would be a telling exercise if we could figure out a way to keep track of how many times we say "yes" to God in a given day or week, especially if we compare it to how many times we say "no." In my life it seems like God has to work for the "yes" sometimes. Do you ever notice how certain ideas or themes come up in your life over and over in a short period of time? Like one day you're reading a blog that brings up the idea of choosing to speak kindly. Then later a song comes on the radio about words that can be hurtful. The next day a friend shares with you that she got in a fight with her daughter and said some harmful things she regrets. Then you go to church and the message is about the James 3 passage on taming the tongue. Maybe now God has your attention!

It's as if God is gently nudging us, begging us for a "yes" at every turn. If we answer with "no," we deprive ourselves of the spiritual formation God had planned. We close ourselves off to what is next. We remain stuck in the ordinary. But if we say, "yes," the door of possibility opens. Our closest relationships are nourished, we unleash the best in those around us and God draws us in to His intentions. And we can be sure that those intentions are very, very good.

The Bible is filled with God's ideas about who we are and what He wants from us. It's also filled with truths about who He is and what He is capable of. These are the realities of relationship with God, and He wants us to say "yes" to these truths. He gives us ample opportunity to respond with a "yes."

He says that I am a new creation. That means the old stuff about me isn't who I am anymore, and the new part of me that came about because of Christ is who I really am. I wonder if I say "yes" to that very often.

He says that I'm alive even when I feel like I'm dead. He tells me that when it comes to my own righteousness I bring nothing to the table, but that the table is already full because He got there first. He tells me that His grace is enough.

Yet, I usually focus a lot on the stuff I should be *doing* instead of resting in the truth that God already did it for me. It's like I'm trying to prove to God that His investment in me was worth it. Or maybe I've thought somewhere in the back of my mind that He's crossing His fingers that I'll turn out OK, and I'm going to show Him that I'm a good kid.

And, He tells me that I can have victory in any situation.

Hmmm…

So, it seems to me that if I would just concentrate on saying "yes" to the reality that He is contributing to the scene of my life, whether it's about who I am or who He is or what He wants from me, I could take huge strides forward in my walk with Him. When my first, instinctual response is "yes" it lays the ground work for where God and I go next. I think what could be built on a foundation like that is a pretty incredible scene of a life…one that I'd like to be a part of.

Chapter 3
Say, "Yes, And..."

Saying "yes" in improvisation gets the ball rolling, but to keep it rolling we add another little, but powerful, word: "and." You didn't see that coming, did you? Not just "yes" but, "Yes, and..." It means that once you've accepted what someone has given you in the scene, you add to it and build the scene. You "and" it.

Let's use the examples from the previous chapter again. If your scene partner just informed you that you are the Queen of Egypt, then, yes, you are the Queen of Egypt and your next move is to "and" the declaration. So you might reply, "Yes, I am the Queen, and my sorcerers tell me that you must not be trusted." Or, "Yes, I am the Queen, and you will be my King!" Or maybe, "Yes, I am the Queen," and then you slap them. As you can see, action can be the "and." The goal is to progress the scene with what you contribute.

There's no wrong reply, as long as you receive what's given with a "yes," (not always verbally but at least implied) and you enhance what's given with an "and" (often verbally, sometimes with action).

We used to play a lot of warm-up games before a show. Mostly it was to be silly, get the energy flowing and connect to each other. But one that I remember was to get us better at incorporating the "and" of "Yes, and..." (I think the exercise was actually called "Yes, And..." You know, for creative people, improvisers come up with pathetic names for stuff.) We all stood in a circle, and the first person would make a statement such as, "I enjoy roller coasters." Then the next person would say, "Yes, and..." and then add something to the statement. We would keep going around the circle until we felt that we got as much as we could out of it.

It would go like this:

1 – I enjoy roller coasters.
2 – Yes, and I've been on 47 since January.

3 – Yes, and I get sick every time.

4 – Yes, and I end up in the Emergency Room.

5 – Yes, and I don't have any insurance.

6 – Yes, and I don't have a job.

7 – Yes, and I live in my car.

8 – Yes, and I'm really enjoying our first date!

Whenever we did this exercise, we ended up in an unexpected place but a creative and unique place that we never would have gotten to without the "and." The "and" is necessary because it elicits collaboration and contribution, two non-negotiable keys to improvisation and two aspects of a relationship with God that are worth discussing.

The previous chapter was about saying "yes" to who God says we are and what He wants from us. To add to that idea, I'm learning that I feel most alive in my relationship with God when I say, "Yes, and…" to Him. It's not that He needs something added, as if what He offers is not enough. Instead it's about the collaboration and contribution that "Yes, and…" brings. The whole idea of relationship is that it's something between two people. I am not the relationship. God is not the relationship. It's what we have between us, the us itself, that is the relationship.

So, what that means is that I don't just receive from God but that I give something back. Now, to be clear, I'm not talking about earning God's forgiveness or pursuing a works-based plan for salvation. What I'm talking about is simply interacting with God. It's realizing that God wants my gifts, strengths, perspective, personality, ideas and resources to be an integral part of how our relationship works. It's knowing that God created me to be unique and that my relationship with Him will not look exactly like anyone else's. Saying, "Yes, and…" to God means that when He gives me an idea of what I'm supposed to be doing, it's up to me to figure out what that can look like.

Imagine two different people, both followers of Christ, both growing in their relationships with God. Imagine they both hear God tell them to help the poor. How they "hear" God doesn't matter, for the sake of this example we can even imagine that He said it out loud. The point here is not how God communicates to us, but rather how we collaborate with Him in the context of our relationship. Ok, now that we have that straight… So they both hear God tell them to help the poor. They both say, "Yes," to God. Then they each say, "And…" as well.

Person #1 finds out about a mission trip to Thailand shortly after hearing from God and feels that the best way to obey God is to participate in the missions work. This is her "Yes, and…" She goes on the trip and feels great affirmation that this was what God wanted from her. Then God communicates that He wants even more from her with helping the poor. This time, her "and" is to return to her church, share with the youth group about her trip and organize a fundraiser to send support to the missionaries she worked with in Thailand.

Person #2 hears from God to help the poor. This guy immediately has a face pop into his mind. It's the face of a homeless guy he sees everyday on his way to work. He decides that the next day he will grab an extra breakfast meal at the drive-thru he frequents a few times a week and give it to the homeless guy. This is what Person #2's "Yes, and…" looks like. So he does just that and feels like it was the right way to obey God. Throughout the day, he keeps thinking about the man and senses that God wants him to do more. So the next day, and in fact that whole week, he brings breakfast to the homeless man. He keeps saying "Yes, and…" to God's nudging, and what results is a unique relationship with a man that he would have otherwise just kept passing by unnoticed.

In both of our imaginary scenarios, God asks something of a believer, and He gets a "yes" from them. They both add an "and" to that but each in a different way, born out of different personalities and different circumstances. The result is as unique as their relationships with God are.

I don't think we can overestimate the importance of saying "Yes, and..." to God. This idea of taking what you've been given and adding to it comes out of a heart that desires to please God. Jesus talks about this very thing in the story of the talents found in Matthew 16. Here's my paraphrase of that story.

A man is going on a journey. So he calls together a few of his employees and hands out some money for them to run things while he's gone. One gets five talents, one gets two and another gets one. The amount doled out was based on how good these guys were at handling the money. After the master leaves, Five-talent Guy immediately starts working to multiply the money and ends up doubling his take. In the same way Two-talent Guy makes another two talents, also doubling what he'd been given. Then we get to One-talent Guy. One-talent Guy is a visionary. He's an entrepreneur. He's...no wait...he buries it in a hole in the ground.

Boss comes back and gathers the guys up to hear the report. First, Five-talent Guy tells how he added to what he'd been given. And he gets a, "Well done, good and faithful servant! You have been faithful with a few things; I will put you in charge of many things. Come and share your master's happiness!" Same thing for Two-talent Guy.

Then we get to One-talent Guy. Poor, pathetic One-talent Guy. After reporting on his progress, here is what the boss replies, "You aren't just lazy, you're wicked! The easy way out would have been to at least put the money in the bank so it would gain some interest. But, no...you didn't even do that! To show you what a big deal this is, I will not only take away what I gave you and entrust it to someone else, but I will remove you altogether." Then he has him thrown out.

What's implied in the boss' response to One-talent Guy is that even if he had added to it in the smallest way possible, that would have gotten him a "Well done." In other words, it would have been enough. Maybe God isn't so concerned with *how* we "Yes, and..." Him, but *that* we do it. Again, it comes back to the heart. Do we have a heart to please God even in the face of fear? Do we let the fear take over and paralyze us from what would otherwise be a creative and unique contribution to what God wants from us? Craig Keener in his New Testament Commentary series says this: "[One-talent Guy] is like too many Christians so overwhelmed by the magnitude of God's task that we put off contributing anything to it."

One of the themes of Jesus' story is that when God entrusts something to you, He is pleased when you put "you" into it and make it more than it was. When One-talent Guy doesn't do this he loses his connection to the boss. Conversely, what the others gain is even greater access to him. They get to celebrate with him and look forward to a future with even more potential for "Well dones." When we "Yes, and..." God we are invited to a deeper relationship with Him. We are invited to celebrate with Him. This is a parable, a story. I'm not saying that if we don't "Yes, and..." then God removes His presence from us or even punishes us. But in the very least there is some sort of reward that is missed.

Our "Yes, and..." to God is how we collaborate with God. It's our actions. It's our response to what He says to us. And what I love the most is that God can handle all of our different "ands." He goes down this trail with each of us, not with pre-determined steps, but with an invitation to us to interact with Him and carve out a path that doesn't look exactly like anyone else's.

Several years ago my husband and I were in the middle of a big decision. The stakes were pretty high in terms of how it would affect our family whether we decided one way or the other. During the time when we were thinking about what God wanted us to do we took a trip to Yosemite that we already had planned.

I have this vivid memory on our last day there where we stopped at an overlook to see the amazing landscape. I wandered a ways away from where my husband Chris was, and as I stared at this very powerful and domineering geography, it reminded me of the Creator that made this. He is solid like these rocks. He doesn't change from day to day. He is there, whether I take time to notice or not.

Then, almost as soon as I had this thought, I had this "God-moment" where I felt God saying to me that His presence, His solid, unchanging, continual presence, would go with us no matter which decision we made. It actually felt like God was saying that the decision was up to me. That either way, as long as we continued to serve Him in ministry, that the decision was up to us. In improv language, I felt God urging me to "and" Him. As if the ball was in our court and our interactive, relational God was just waiting to see what we would do.

I don't know if you've ever experienced anything like that, but for me a great weight was lifted that moment. There was a sense of freedom in my heart about the decision. It helped me to realize this truth; God wants me to bring all that I am to our relationship, and together we will maneuver this life that He gave me.

Chapter 4
Give Gifts, Accept Gifts

One of the things I love about improvisation is that at its core it is about ensemble. It happens in a group. And any time you have a group, you have a myriad of ideas, perceptions, opinions, feelings and beliefs. It's from this wealth of diversity that contributions to the scene are made. Dialogue between the characters is really just a volley back and forth of the improvisers' ideas and contributions. You begin to give of yourself and your partner gets the opportunity to accept what you've given. And vice versa. In improvisation we call this giving each other "gifts."

If Joe and Sally are in a scene, and Joe tells Sally that he's just finished an online course in flying and she's about to be his first passenger, he's given Sally a gift, a gift of information. Her scene partner just informed her about his character, his goals and his hopes as well as given her a specific emotional tension to which she can now respond. Internet flying lessons, scary! Sally's job, now, is to accept that gift from Joe and give him a gift back. She might say something like, "That's amazing, Joe. I've been meaning to tell you something lately but just haven't worked up the courage. Being stuck in a cockpit together at 10,000 feet should do the trick!" Joe accepts Sally's gift. Sally has a secret that she is going to tell him, and the scene goes on in the same pattern. Each actor/character gives and receives gifts until an unplanned, organic scene unfolds. Probably one where they both die at the end, because, hey, what do you expect from a sham pilot and an emotionally unstable girl?

Getting back to the idea of group, what's cool about this gift giving and accepting is that you fully embrace what the other group members offer you, and you know that they will fully embrace what you give back. You can give uniquely, because you are unique. And it's up to everyone around you to receive it. Then *together* you can create the scene.

One of the reasons I think this improvisational concept excites me so much is that there is a spiritual parallel I'm passionate about. Just as we contribute gifts to the scene in improvisation, as believers we have spiritual gifts to contribute to the world around us. Nothing energizes me more than using my spiritual gifts and helping other people find ways to use theirs. I really believe, to the core of who I am, that God designed each of us with something to give, something to contribute to His work in the world. Conversely, I also believe we are all destined to receive something priceless when the people around us use their gifts.

The Bible tells us, "Each of you should use whatever gift you have received to serve others, as faithful stewards of God's grace in its various forms." (1 Peter 4:10) It also teaches that God's church is like a body, every part has a purpose and no part is unimportant (1 Corinthians 12).

My undergrad studies were in biology, and just before my senior year of college, I started to feel God calling me to ministry instead of medicine. I spent the first half of my last year in college trying to sort out what God wanted me to do at this critical crossroads in my life. It was a definite redirection from the trajectory I was on. By January of that year I felt fully affirmed that God wanted me to pursue a life of ministry. As I completed my college degree in biology, I began to put some plans in motion for what I would do next. I applied and was accepted to Fuller Theological Seminary in Pasadena and moved my entire life there the next fall.

When my fellow biology nerd friends were heading off to micro-biology programs in Colorado, pursuing teaching credentials and starting physical therapy internships, I was signing up for classes like "Old Testament Survey" and "Patristic Theology." I know...you're jealous! It was a weird time for me because I was closing the door on a subject that was fascinating and made sense to me, and I was pursuing something that felt like foreign territory, academically speaking at least.

Now while I'm sure you want to hear more about my exciting seminary classes, let me fast forward...years later, when I wasn't really expecting it, I discovered what God had in store for me all along. He wanted me to equip believers to understand and engage in being the part of the body God created them to be. When I first went to Fuller and people asked what my undergrad studies were in, they would look at me funny when I said biology. (Or they were looking at me funny because I still had acne, I mean let's face it folks, acne is hilarious!) So my standard line became, "Well, I already studied the body so now I'm studying the spirit!"

But now I know (and forgive me because this is going to sound really cheesy) that when God called me to ministry, it wasn't a call away from studying the "body." I think that's why I'm so drawn to the idea that the church is the body of Christ, and each of us is a significant, useful, irreplaceable part of that body. In anatomy, each body part is integrally related to all the others. I love that as a whole the body is a highly functioning entity because of the individual parts. And I love that Christ designed the Church to be the same way.

Spiritually speaking, we all have gifts to contribute, like encouragement, mercy, leadership or teaching, and the church only achieves its potential as its people are serving one another and the world around them by using the gifts God gave them. Once you believe that you have something to offer, that in fact, He has given you something to offer, there is this confidence and satisfaction that resides deep in your soul. And it's not a prideful, selfish realization but a humble, grateful discovery that God wants to use you.

Using our gifts will look different from one person to the next. First of all, each of us has a different set of gifts that work together creating unique abilities, all of which flow through our unique personality. So, even if I have similar gifts to you, it won't look the same when we use them. Imagine someone who has a gift of encouragement and also has an outgoing, gregarious personality. When they are encouraging someone, it will most likely be in a highly relational and interactive context, probably in a very long conversation over coffee. On the other hand, for someone with the same gift but a more reserved relational style, encouraging others would more likely come through small, intentional encouragements over a long period of time. It might even come by way of a handwritten note or an e-mail. Same gift. Same effectiveness. Different style.

Secondly, the context in which we use our gifts is also unique. Usually when we read about spiritual gifts in the Bible, it's in reference to God-given abilities that are to be used to build up the church. It's important to realize that our gifts may manifest themselves differently depending on the particular church in which we take part. But if we believe that God has called us to a certain church then tandem with that call is, I believe, an expectation that we will use our gifts in the context of ministry there. When we contribute in this way to our local church (church with a small "c"), we are by definition building up the Church (church with a big "C") as well. The bottom line is that our church (or our group, our family or our relationships) won't fully be what they can be until we are each submitting our gifts to the greater good of the larger whole. And when that happens...the sky's the limit! I believe that's what God had in mind all along.

Hebrews 11 is a running list of great people of faith from Abel to the martyrs of the early church. I first learned about this chapter in the Bible when I was in third grade. It was part of the curriculum at my little Christian school to memorize this chapter. Since that time, Hebrews 11 has always been a little bit intimidating to me. Here are these spiritual giants and faithful heroes who literally made history. Those are big footsteps to walk in! But recently I came across the last two verses of the chapter, and they gave me a new perspective on the whole chapter. They read:

> "These were all commended for their faith, yet none of them received what had been

promised. God had planned something better for us so that only together with us would they be made perfect." (Hebrews 11:39-40)

These verses are an affirmation that every one of us counts and was created to be a part of something bigger than ourselves. I know that ultimately this verse refers to heaven, but I find that it reveals something about God when it comes to His Church. Our individual faith empowers us to contribute to His story uniquely, and ultimately we are creating the Church together with God. So as we give our gifts and *because* we do, we get to live out the ending that He promised.

So I give my gift and you give yours, and I receive yours and you receive mine, until a scene unfolds that none of us could have expected. In the middle of it all we become the ensemble that God had in mind because, by the way, He's not making it up as He goes along.

Chapter 5
Don't Ask Questions

One of the most basic improvisation rules that a budding improv artist learns, even in their very first class is "Don't Ask Questions." In fact, whenever I taught the beginner class at the improv training center, I literally did teach this in the very first class. "What do you mean?" you say. I said don't ask questions.

Seriously, though, in an improvised scene you don't know any more about where the scene is going than your audience does. And you don't really know who you are or who your partner is, so it comes very natural to just ask questions like:

Why are you so afraid of heights?

What's behind your back?

Do you think we should open this letter?

But there's a problem with questions. They don't move the scene forward. In improvisation, ideally, whenever someone speaks they have added to the scene. Maybe they've made a new statement about someone's character or how they feel about a situation or what they are doing. Essentially, each line is giving information to the audience as well as the people in the scene. A question doesn't usually give information, and it tends to stall the scene.

Here's an example. Instead of saying, "Hey, do you think we should open this letter?" you said, "I know this letter says 'Confidential,' but Grandpa's will is inside, and before the rest of the family arrives I want to know what I'm getting!" Now all of a sudden we have some juicy information, and we can't wait to see what happens next. Much more fun!

In fairness, not all questions are bad. A question like, "Will you marry me?" can significantly move the scene forward. But often, quite often, when an improviser asks a question it's because they don't know where to take the scene. Asking a question buys them time. It's a way to stall.

As you know by now, this book uses improvisation rules as a metaphor for our relationship with God. So there's probably no big surprise that

I'm going to suggest that maybe we stop asking God so many questions. But before I go there, let me just say that I don't think asking God questions is wrong. In fact, it's necessary. It's beneficial to any relationship. It's foundational in the getting-to-know-you process. I'd go so far as to say that without questions there's not much of a relationship at all!

I have this pet peeve about people I meet who don't ask questions. Do you know the kind of people I'm talking about? You're trying to get to know them so you ask them questions about their life, their family, their job, their hobbies, etc. This is how you convey interest. So it seems logical to me, that if someone wants to get to know me they might ask me a question or two. Maybe I'm assuming too much. Maybe they don't want to get to know me. Which brings me to my second pet peeve: I hate when people don't want to get to know me! Seriously, though, questions are non-negotiable in relationship.

One of my friends is married to a guy that is ultra shy. He hardly talks at all. He could go through a whole night at a party and say about 10 words. So when you're talking to him one-on-one you have to work pretty hard to keep the conversation going. One night when a group of our friends went out, he ended up sitting right across from me. I was making my usual effort to make up for the fact that he wasn't saying much, when suddenly he surprised me with a question. A real question! An actual attempt to drive the conversation forward!

Here I was thinking that I would never have a two-sided conversation with this guy, and then he goes and asks a question. He was making an effort, and I was thrilled. Unfortunately, about three seconds after he asked the question the conversation died outright.

Me: So, that's about all we did this weekend.

(awkward pause)

Him: Uh huh.

(another awkward pause)

Me: Yep. That and a little TV.

(looks at me)

Him: Hey, do you watch Survivor?

(No way...he's asking a question! This is great!)

Me: Yeah. Do you?

(We'll have something to talk about for months!)

Him: No...I'm not really into reality TV.

(This is going to be a long night.)

So what I'm trying to say is that questions are necessary. They are one of the ingredients to a flourishing relationship, and it's no different with God. He made us as finite people who don't know the answers. So, of course, questions are integral to our spiritual process.

What I am noticing, though, is that sometimes questions can stall us. It's easy to get obsessive about asking God for details like, "Should I do this or that?" or, "Do you want me to go here or there?" And our tendency can be that we ask so many questions we fail to get on with the *action*. I think God wisely chooses to operate on a need-to-know basis with us much of the time, and in so doing, He only lets us in on one piece of the puzzle. These stalling questions are usually about our frustration with the pieces of the puzzle that He has not chosen to reveal yet.

I think of Moses when God first called him to return to Egypt and confront Pharaoh. Here's what we see Moses asking and how God responded (You'll notice I have taken some creative liberties with God's internal dialogue. But otherwise the conversation is pretty true to the biblical text.):

God : I have heard the cries of my people enslaved in Egypt, and I am ready to help them. I'm sending you to Pharaoh so I can free My people.

God (to Himself): The time has come. This is a great moment! 400 years in the making. I'm ready to make My move!

Moses: Who am I, that I should go to Pharaoh and bring the Israelites out of Egypt?

God (to Himself): OK, I guess that's a fair
  question.

God: Don't worry, Moses. I'll be with
  you. I promise this is going to work
  out.

Moses: What if they ask me who sent me?
  What am I supposed to say then?

God (to Himself): I'm sensing some
  hesitancy. Let me be a little more
  clear....

God: Tell them I AM sent you.

(blank stare from Moses)

God: Then they'll know that I sent you.
  Here's exactly what you should do.
  Tell them who I am, gather the
  leaders together and remind them
  of My promise. They will listen to
  you. Then you're going to go to

Pharaoh and ask for a three-day pass. He'll refuse, and then I'll end up causing a lot of problems for him and his country. Finally I will win, and My people will be free. And I'll even up the ante: Just to show you I am in control, when you do leave, you'll leave with loads of gold and riches straight from the hands of the Egyptians.

God (to Himself): OK...that oughta do it. Now let's get going.

Moses: What if they don't believe me? What if they don't even listen to me or if they accuse me of lying about You sending me to them?

God (to Himself): This is going to be a long night.

(So, God does some miracles for Moses and tells him He'll repeat those same miracles in front of the people if they have a hard time believing God sent him.)

God: And hey, Moses, even if by some crazy chance that still doesn't work, take some water from the Nile and pour it out. I'll turn it to blood right before their eyes. It'll be great!

Moses: How is this going to work? I'm not good at talking in front of people. Do You realize I am not a good communicator?

God: Yes I know that.

Moses: Can you send someone else?

("Then the Lord's anger burned against Moses." Exodus 4:14)

God: Fine...how about your brother Aaron?

Moses' questions came from a place of fear, doubt and uncertainty. And I can just picture him standing there, kind of dumbstruck with question after question because God wasn't giving him all the information he felt like he needed before he could move forward.

But here's the thing: God was giving him what God wanted to give him! I think He wanted Moses to trust Him. God knew what lay ahead for their relationship and was probably trying to establish some groundwork for what was to come. Instead of trust He got doubt. Instead of action He got questions. Moses seemed to be stalling.

And it looks like it didn't stop after the burning bush. If you keep reading in Exodus 4, you see that Moses gathers up his family and begins the journey to Egypt. Then we get to this crazy verse that seems to come out of nowhere. It says, "At a lodging place on the way, the Lord met Moses and was about to kill him." (Exodus 4:25)

I'm wondering if it was because he wouldn't shut up with the questions! (Note: Every commentary I read suggests that God's immense anger had more to do with Moses neglecting to circumcise his son, but there could have been more than one reason, right?)

Here's the deal. I'm not saying that Moses' questions weren't legit. His whole world was about to get turned upside down and there was a very real chance (at least from his perspective) that he could end up humiliated, enslaved or even dead. But don't you kind of sense that God was getting a little irritated at his many questions? Probably not so much because they were unreasonable, but because at their core they told God there was unbelief. And at the heart of it all, God was asking for belief: belief that He had not forgotten His promise to His people, belief that He was big enough, belief that nothing was impossible.

That is still what He wants from us.

Our belief.

Often our questions stem from a sincere desire to clearly understand who God is and what He wants from us. They deepen our relationships with Him. They show we're seeking His will, and we want to follow Him. These are the right questions. But other times, our questions are simply a stalling tactic that we mutter as we stare dumbfounded at our burning bush. We ask, "What about…" and, "What if…" and,

"How can I..." in an effort to satisfy what we think we need to know from God before we can move forward.

I wonder if we could silence these kinds of questions. I think it would be worth it to try. Because at the heart of the unasked question is a heart that is choosing to believe. And you'd be amazed at what God can do with a heart like that.

Chapter 6
Turn Off Your Filter

A lot can happen in a second. A human heart will beat once. You will blink two to three times. A hummingbird will flap its wings up to 80 times. A cheetah will run more than 100 feet. 150,000 gallons of water will cascade over the crest of the Niagara Falls. A lot can happen in a second. The same is true of improvisation. In fact, a lot must happen in a second. In that short moment of time, scenes are started, characters are created, relationships are formed and the foundation for tension in a scene is laid...all in about a second.

Because of the speedy nature of improvisation, a good improviser must respond quickly. There is not a lot of time for contemplation, so you pretty much have to go with your first instinct. When you are in a scene and an idea pops into your head, you don't have the luxury of thinking it over and deciding if it's a good idea or not. Usually, you just spit it out and go with it. You don't question it, and you know that your scene partner won't question it either. They will just respond and react to what you bring.

I'm one of those people whose mouth is about three steps ahead of her brain. More often than not a remark comes out of my mouth that just shouldn't be said out loud. Now don't get me wrong, everyone else was thinking it too, it's just that they all have this thing called "the filter." I used to have it. Then I started doing improv.

In improvisation, you must turn off that filter that we all have in regular life. It's the filter that tells us when something is a dumb idea, and we shouldn't suggest it. It's what helps us know what is appropriate to say. The filter helps us form our words and change our tone so that we don't offend people. It also inhibits us from doing anything that will make us look bad.

It takes time to develop this filter. Kids usually don't have it. Kids say things like, "Mommy your tummy is fat. Is there another baby in there?" I'm just making that up, of course. Totally hypothetical. Not a personal example.

So, most of us have this filter, and thank goodness. Filter equals ability to function as a healthy person in society.

But with improvisation, part of the fun and really the entire foundation of it, is that you don't know where it will take you because there's no filter. You learn to ignore it and render it powerless to inhibit you in any way, shape or form. That sounds dangerous and scary, and to be honest, it is! But when I learned how to perform without a filter onstage, I began to see what could happen. One time I started performing an impromptu gymnastics routine in a scene. The filter would have said, "You don't know anything about gymnastics. Was that supposed to be a cartwheel? This is not going to end well." But before I could heed the filter, my partner exclaimed, "Eugenia, you're legs have been healed!" And the scene evolved into a touching but hilarious tale about a poor colonial family who invented a miracle elixir that made them rich. It was so very worth it when I got to the other side of it all and was able to experience something we never could have planned.

In improvisation turning off the filter means you listen to your gut and move forward with the action even when you don't know what the outcome will look like. In our spiritual lives, turning off the filter means you listen to the Holy Spirit and move forward with the action even when you don't know what the outcome will look like. I think we all have a spiritual filter. The filter I'm talking about comes from doubt, fear and confusion, and it causes us to shut out what the Holy Spirit might be moving us to do. As believers, the Holy Spirit shows us how to live our life in a way that brings glory to God. There is this ongoing communication from the Spirit leading us to a God-filled life. Galatians 5:22 puts it this way, "Since we live by the Spirit, let us keep in step with the Spirit." I believe the Holy Spirit impresses His ideas onto our hearts in order to drive us to do something godly that we might not have otherwise done. In other words, the Holy Spirit keeps up His end of the deal when it comes to leading us.

But when it comes to following Him, we all have this filter that questions what we hear. When God brings an idea to mind, such as "Send this money to the earthquake relief," or "Spend some extra time with your spouse today," or "Offer to pray for that stranger in distress," the filter clicks on.

Remember, the filter is the logical part of us

that evaluates if something is really a good idea or not. The problem with this on a spiritual level is that many of God's ideas don't seem like good ones at the time. We read about the people in the Bible who were on the receiving end of ideas like this. To Moses He said, "Go back to that land you left as a fugitive and demand freedom from the most powerful ruler on earth." To Gideon He said, "32,000 reluctant soldiers seems like too many for an attack on the oppressive Midianite army, so let's take it down to, I don't know...300...ah...that's better." To Peter, "Start preaching to the Gentiles, yeah, those un-Kosher, unholy, seemingly unchosen people. Tell them that My grace is for them, too." You get the point. The inspiring stories of the Bible are catapulted into reality because someone turned off their filter and just did what God was prompting them to do. Whether it made perfect sense to them or not was beside the point.

Their fear in the middle of it all was also beside the point. I think fear is a very real facet of the kind of action that God prompts us to take. Nelson Mandela said, "I learned that courage was not the absence of fear, but the triumph over it. The brave man is not he who does not feel afraid, but he who conquers that fear." As we listen and respond to the promptings of the Holy Spirit, we are bound to experience fear; fear that we will fail, fear that we will look foolish, fear that we are hearing Him incorrectly, you name it. But in order for us to be responsive to God, we often have to turn off this filter or at the very least, ignore it.

When we don't do this we run the risk of getting stagnant in our walk and bored with our relationship with Jesus. It's usually not because we aren't given opportunities to do the exciting. It's because we filter them out before they have a chance to take root in our lives and grow into something worthwhile. And the result is that we begin to feel like our side of the relationship falls flat.

But when we ditch the filter, well, that's a whole different story.

In 2 Thessalonians 1:11-12 Paul writes, "We constantly pray for you, that our God may make you worthy of His calling, and that by His power He may bring to fruition your every desire for goodness and your every deed prompted by faith. We pray this so that the name of our Lord Jesus may be glorified in you, and you in Him, according to the grace of our God and the Lord Jesus Christ."

I want my "every desire for goodness" and "every deed prompted by faith" to come to fruition. I truly believe that God is still in the business of speaking to us and, in fact, it is because He is alive in us that a "deed prompted by faith" can even exist. But communication is never a one-way street, so we must become listeners to the One who prompts us. And as we do we must refuse to let our only filter be the "what-makes-sense-to-me" filter.

Now don't get me wrong. There are filters that God *wants* us to use, filters that tell us if it's Him in the first place. John Ortberg talks about this in his book "If You Want to Walk on Water, You've Got to Get Out of the Boat." He says, "Knowing when to...take a risk does not only demand courage, it also demands the wisdom to ask the right questions, the discernment to recognize the voice of the Master, and the patience to wait for His command."

I love that description. It epitomizes the balance of a wise risk. But notice that what Ortberg does not include in his list is "the comfort of knowing that the plan makes sense to me." It's not always part of the criteria. God just doesn't seem to work that way. 1 Corinthians 1:25-29 says,

"For the foolishness of God is wiser than human wisdom, and the weakness of God is stronger than human strength. Brothers and sisters, think of what you were when you were called. Not many of you were wise by human standards; not many were influential; not many were of noble birth. But God chose the foolish things of the world to shame the wise; God chose the weak things of the world to shame the strong. God chose the lowly things of this world and the despised things—and the things that are not—to nullify the things that are, so that no one may boast before Him."

As we seek to be people that know Him, we must practice taking steps of obedience in the small things even when we don't know why God might be moving us in that direction. That way when we get to the big things, the things that are *way* out of our comfort zone, we will move to action when we hear God's still small voice.

Chapter 7
Heighten the Scene

When you are watching a movie, there is usually a point where you become invested in the story enough that there is now no turning back. You hit that place where you absolutely have to know what happens next. You've been hooked. This happens with books, magazine articles and even news stories. There is a point that we as the audience or reader start to "buy in" to what's happening in the story. It's a component in any good story, really. You start to identify with the character, or you have a strong emotional reaction to the story's content. I don't think, subjectively speaking, that a story can be interesting unless there is this buy-in.

I've never liked coming-of-age movies. When they end I tend to find myself disappointed that there wasn't more to it. Don't get me wrong, I know there can be something poignant and even inspiring in these stories. Chris is a fan, so usually when we are talking about a movie afterwards he tries to convince me how great it was and explain all the nuances to me. I guess I'm just not much into subtleties. But here's my real problem...I just don't care. No offense to the kid who grew up in a small town, but had big dreams and overcame his fear of crowds in order to win the big boat race. It feels like something is missing - some emotional tug that I don't get.

In improvisation, we intentionally try to create that tug, to get our audience to buy in to our story. We do that by "heightening the scene." Heightening is creating an imaginary reality that people start to care about. It's the last chance at love. It's the "all in" bet. It's the reveal of a deathbed secret. Like any story, it might be content driven or character driven, but either way the listener connects in an emotional way to what's going on. It's called heightening because the characters build the scene one layer at a time until it has the audience's complete attention. The stakes are high. The anticipation is high. And you watch with raised eyebrows to see how it will all turn out.

Achieving height in an improvised scene can be tricky because you go about it in sort of an indirect way. Instead of aiming at making it "bigger and better" you aim at going deeper and more realistic. When you do that, the bigger and better comes on its own, and the scene is heightened naturally. Here's the difference:

> Scene 1: The butler runs wildly into the crowded parlor, flailing his arms and shouting, "Mr. Dunsworth has been murdered, and there's a killer on the loose!" Then he points dramatically at Mr. Barnes and shouts, "You!"

In this scene the butler character tries to heighten the scene by being over the top and exclamatory. What he's created, however, is a short-lived emotional peak. He superficially manufactured a climax instead of letting it crescendo from a grounded, authentic place. Imagine if the scene looked like this instead:

> Scene 2 : The butler walks somberly into the crowded parlor. In a voice just above a

whisper he says, "There's been a murder." Then with no bodily movement other than his eyes, he looks accusingly at Mr. Barnes.

Here the heightening is more powerful and effective. It is tangible because it was grounded in realism. It wasn't forced. Because the butler patiently resided in the matter-of-fact, the scene is primed for fantastic heights.

Liz used to be an engineer. So she is a creative, artistic person who is also secretly a math nerd. As only an improviser/engineer could, she explained "heightening" using an invisible sine wave chart. Remember sine waves from trigonometry? They look like this:

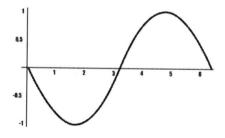

A sine wave is a pattern that we see occurring often in nature. Ocean waves, light waves and sounds waves all follow this down-up pattern. What we see in sine waves is however low they sink below the midline is equal distance to how high they rise above it.

One night at rehearsal Liz walked over to the wall, reached into the air and made the motion of pulling down a screen. Again, hearkening back to when you were in school, remember all the maps and screens that your teacher had above the chalkboard? Your teacher would pull down whichever one she needed at the time: map of the world, map of the U.S., projector screen, etc. But she would inevitably pull the wrong one down first and then have to do that quick "pull and release" maneuver to make it go back up. Of course, then it always got stuck. It's sad that that is one of my clearest memories of elementary school. So anyway, Liz pulls down her imaginary screen at rehearsal. If I remember right, she actually pulled down the wrong invisible screen first and had to switch it...improviser's sense of humor.

She explained the sine wave chart to us by saying,

"The sine wave can only go as high as it goes low, and vice versa. If it is a shallow wave, it stays a shallow wave throughout. If it has depth, then it also has height. The same is true in your scenes.

"If you are willing to be vulnerable in your characters and in your relationships, if you are willing to go to the depths of revealing truth and taking risks, then and only then, will your relationships reach full height.

"And it is at that height, and only there, that you find satisfaction as an improviser. It's where you reach the funniest humor and where you find the greatest 'Aha!' moments with each other and with your audience. You cannot manufacture the height. It must come as an inverse reaction to the depth."

When you see improvisers live this out in their scene creation, it's like nothing else you've ever witnessed. As an audience you go with them to this vulnerable, sometimes embarrassing and often awkward reality, and then like a slingshot pulled back to it's full tautness, you go flying to the very fulfilling, adrenaline-filled and (usually) hilarious ending. All because you were willing to go to the depths.

"Middle of the road," "mediocre," "take it or leave it;" these are not comments an improviser would like to have said about their scene. I would venture to say that these are also not the kind of words that we would like to have said about our lives. We long for the fantastic outcome, but are often unwilling to go to the depths: the scary place, the unknown place and the place of greatest risk and vulnerability. We instinctively know that this is also the place where the most severe failure is possible.

I'm always a little jealous of people who have these incredible God-experiences. Like the ones where someone is literally down to their last dollar and that day they get an unexpected check in the mail. Several years ago I was reading a book about George Muller. He was an evangelist in the 1800s who is most remembered for his work with children, specifically orphans. Through starting and overseeing numerous orphanages in England, he was able to touch the lives of more than 10,000 children. What I remember most about the book and about Muller's life was that he *continually* heightened his faith. His orphanages were constantly struggling financially, and he would make huge asks of God through prayer, usually not even telling anyone else about his prayer. He believed that the request needed to be between just him and God, and God would take care of his needs without Muller even needing to make the request to anyone else. Time and time again, as Muller put himself out there with God as his only safety net, he was given exactly what was needed.

On one occasion, all the children in one of the orphan houses (usually several hundred at each orphanage) were seated waiting to eat breakfast. The only problem was that there was no food for the children to eat. I don't know about you but in my house if there's not a plethora of breakfast choices there's practically a mutiny! But these children were all sitting there with empty stomachs and empty plates. Muller, true to form, insisted they all pray for the food. I love this picture. Can you imagine? "Thank you, Lord, for this food...except, wait, there isn't any food...awkward!" But, as they finished praying they heard a knock at the door. It was a baker delivering enough bread for everyone. Say what??

The entire book is filled with stories just like this. Here was a man who followed God in a big, daring way. He wasn't afraid of hardship, because he knew God could reverse it. And as this spiritual upswing occurred again and again for Muller, he was able to make an indelible mark on thousands of children's lives.

I think we are drawn to the stories of great loss, great victory, great cost or beating the odds because deep inside of us we long for that emotional and spiritual euphoria that only comes when great risk is taken. We care more when the stakes are high because we know that while the loss might be devastating, the reward is unparalleled. Helen Keller said, "Life is either a daring adventure or nothing." We were created to live a life that is a daring adventure.

We see great adversity and great adventures all throughout the Bible as well. In Luke, Jesus meets a woman who was a prostitute, and He noticed not her blatant failure but her sincere love.

"Therefore, I tell you, her many sins have been forgiven—for she loved much. But he who has been forgiven little loves little." (Luke 7:47)

Great failure. Great love.

The name Job. Say no more. Well, maybe say "Why is there no 'e' at the end of this name?" Let's be honest...it's confusing! But other than that, say no more. Job experienced devastating loss. And after the loss, "The Lord blessed the latter part of Job's life more than the first." (Job 42:12)

Great loss. Great reward.

When I think of the person in the Bible that probably had the most skeletons in his closet I think of Paul. We've gotten to know him through the pages of Scripture that the Holy Spirit used him to write. But the Paul that we've seen has been on our side. He was a vital force in the early church. Arguably, he was the strongest influence, aside from Christ, in all of Christendom. But what we see is a result of the upswing of Paul's spiritual sine wave.

Prior to his conversion he was running full force, guns blazing in the direction he thought God wanted, only to find out that he had it all wrong, and in the process had made some irreversible mistakes. Saul/Paul strikes me as a man who "goes big or goes home" regardless of what side he's on. Of course, God saw all that in him. So He pointed out to Paul that he needed to change the course of his life, and by "pointed out" I mean: ambushed him on the road to Damascus, charged him with persecuting Jesus Himself, struck him blind and left him flat on his face unable to eat or drink for three days. (I love how subtle God is sometimes.) Those three days changed Paul's trajectory. BAM! His potential for good was unleashed.

Great mistakes. Great impact.

I see these same sine wave patterns when I look at the people around me today. My staff colleague at church is a tireless caregiver, equipping others to tangibly come alongside anyone who has a need. Where does this come from? It comes out of her past when she did not get this kind of support while struggling through an abusive marriage.

My friend Tim is wholeheartedly committed to a God-honoring attitude about money. He used to be money driven and money obsessed. About five years ago he was well on his way to becoming a millionaire "ahead of schedule" until a dishonest investment manager took advantage of him. He walked away with a bundle of Tim's money, to the tune of about $500,000. Financially, emotionally and spiritually he hit rock bottom. But it was there that God changed him. Through the devastation he recognized the hold money had on his life. He began to learn on a spiritual level how God wanted him to handle his finances. Today he is passionate about teaching others how to have the right perspective when it comes to their money. He is committed to helping others overcome their preoccupation with money and gain a healthy spiritual view of their resources.

I see it in my friend Sarah who rescues women from the red light district in India near Calcutta. She runs a business that is part of an organization called Word Made Flesh. Her business, Sari Bari, offers women working in the sex trade employment as seamstresses. They make handbags and quilts from Indian saris. These beautiful pieces are then distributed locally and globally through their website www.saribari.com. (Feel free to stop reading now if you want to go order something from her website. I'll be here when you get back.) Her ministry is the very definition of incarnational ministry. She and the other Sari Bari leaders reside just on the edge of the sex district. For the past six years, they have spent thousands of hours walking the local streets bringing love, acceptance and friendship to the women in these dire straights.

As you can imagine, the level of despair she sees on a daily basis is overwhelming. The hopelessness and desperation are palpable. She writes about it saying, "The assault on human dignity is devastating...and yet we cling to the hope that the women of [the red light district] can have freedom, that dignity can be restored, and the streets which are lined with women in slavery can be made new. We believe and are seeing that Jesus makes life new for the women and their families."

The first year Sari Bari employed three women. The next year eight more women came on board. Currently there are two locations employing 70 women, 70 lives that are being transformed from bondage to freedom, in every sense of the word. Sarah continues reaching out to women still ensconced in prostitution, with hopes of one day hearing them accept her invitation to leave their life of slavery. And because of this she perpetually sees and feels the unbearable suffering all around her. But when she returns from the streets back to Sari Bari she has only to look around and know that there is great cause for celebration. Shame has turned into forgiveness. Despair has become hope. Brokenness has made a way for healing. Darkness has been exposed to light. And bondage has been replaced with freedom.

From the depths, great things have arisen.

So for us, here, today...this is what I'm trying to say: don't be afraid of your past because your greatest mistakes can become powerful tools in God's hands. Don't be afraid of your failures because when you've been forgiven much you will love much. Don't be afraid of authentic vulnerability in your relationships because only then will true intimacy be found. Don't be afraid to risk to follow God because the reward will be worth it.

I suppose it's unfair to simply say, "Don't be afraid." It's not like we can really control our emotions, right? But what you can do when you are in the middle of the fear is look hope right in the face, knowing that the upswing is coming because that's just how it works with God. You cannot manufacture the height. It will come as an inverse reaction to the depth.

Chapter 8
The Back Line Players Aren't Taking a Break

Have you ever been in a place in life where you just felt like you had nothing to contribute to the world around you? You look at the people in your life and see that they are growing, learning and influencing. But for you, none of this is happening. We've somehow created these markers for ourselves that we use to evaluate how well we're doing in life. I wonder, though, if these markers have hijacked our spiritual growth on some level, and unless we redefine them we'll continue to miss out on what God's trying to do in us.

Many of our shows at The Second City involved a set of scenes called the "Commando Set."

During Commando the entire cast was onstage, and one of us would ask for some sort of suggestion from the audience. We might ask, "What's a present you got as a kid?" or, "Where's your favorite vacation spot?" or "What's the last purchase you made?" Once we got a suggestion, a couple of us would step out and start a scene inspired by the suggestion. Whoever didn't step out stayed at the back of the stage. These people were referred to as the "back line."

Just hearing the term "back line" makes you think those people are the ones who are not involved in what's happening onstage. They are in the back, after all. And, while that makes sense, it wasn't true in Commando.

In fact, the players on the back line were crucial to the scene that was taking place. The back line players were responsible for two critical jobs. First, they would be the ones that called "scene," when the improvised scene reached its end. The "end" was always subjective because there was no script. It was imperative for the back line players to be listening and engaged in the scene, so they ended the scene at the best possible spot. Someone on the back line would yell "scene" and it would be over.

The second job of those on the back line was to

join into the scene, if the scene called for it. Sometimes a new character would be introduced, sometimes an inanimate object or an animal, or sometimes the back line players were needed to make someone fly. (See "It's Not Impossible to Fly.") Whenever they felt prompted to do so, a player not in the scene could walk into the scene and become part of the action.

One time I was in a scene on a "deserted island." At some point in the scene I admitted a debilitating fear of snakes, and the scene continued. About 15 seconds later my partner looked wild-eyed at the floor behind me. I slowly turned around to a sea of venomous snakes (a.k.a. three members of our cast slithering around on the floor making hissing sounds). We then proceeded to fight off the snakes. I think we tried charming them, but to no avail. Luckily, we were saved by a rabid gorilla (a.k.a. the other member of our cast who was still on the back line). It was a touching and heartfelt scene, as you can imagine. Nonetheless, it was a fun and creative scene because the back line players joined the action.

The back line players had a job to do. They weren't just on pause, waiting it out.

I believe this model can help us understand how

God works in our lives and what He might be expecting from us when He does. Just because you're not in the scene doesn't mean that you are not important to the scene. Translation: just because you feel that God is moving, working or taking action in someone else's life and not yours, it doesn't mean that God has your life on pause.

In 2008 my family relocated to the San Francisco Bay Area. This was a big time of transition in my life. I was in a new city, a new church, a new house, a new school for my daughter, and I had a new daughter on the way. Chris, was in a new ministry role, and for the first time in a long time, I didn't have a paying job. I resigned myself to be in "transition" mode. I knew it would take time for me to make new friends and get myself adjusted to a whole new life. So, I decided to wait it out.

A few months after we moved I went on our church's women's retreat. Little did I know that what God would reveal to me that weekend would turn my whole waiting strategy upside-down. During some free time, I took my Bible and my notebook to a place by the beach where I could sit by myself and "hear from God."

And I heard from God.

In a nutshell, this is what He said:

"You are acting as if I have you in some sort of a holding pattern and you are waiting for the go ahead to land. And I know you will keep waiting until you hear from me, because you think that's what I want from you. But you're going about this all wrong. I have a purpose for you right now. Not just later. Now.

"I'm asking you to open yourself up to what I need to teach you in this season of life where you are feeling purposeless. There is a purpose. There is a great and specific purpose to the now: It is to prepare for what is to come.

"Stop seeing this as transition, and begin to see this as a time of rest where I can invest in you. I'm going to expect big things from you here soon, but you won't have the fortitude to accomplish much if you continue to just hang out waiting for something to happen.

"You must shift your perspective so that I can actively engage you for the plans I've set in motion. Let me do this. You won't regret it."

And just like that, my perspective shifted from one of waiting to one of preparation and action. I no longer felt that I was waiting for God to get around to me and start working in my life. I realized that this "back line" season of my life wasn't a big pause button at all. In fact, it was a time where God was asking me to be engaged and purposeful in my life.

One area where I felt this most strongly was in my time with Quinn, my older daughter. It hit me that this was the last time I would ever have just her. Little sister was on the way and life would never be the same. So I committed to really investing in my time with Quinn. I went out of my way to play with her and take her fun places and just be with her. I'll never forget that I was sitting on the floor with Quinn playing Legos when I went into labor. It felt like a sweet little affirmation from God that I did what He asked. (Well, between contractions it felt like that.) God was very specific about what He wanted from me, and it strengthened Quinn's and my relationship so that we were prepared for baby Kennedy to join the family.

I began to look at ministry differently, too. I knew that I couldn't commit to a long-term volunteer role, because I'd just have to take a break when Kennedy was born, so I felt that my only option was to wait (there's that word again!) to be involved. But, in keeping with what God wanted from me, He provided a serving opportunity that was integral in my preparation for what was coming next.

One of the pastors asked me to teach a spiritual gifts class. The class would only meet once, which worked perfectly for me. I put effort and planning into my preparation, but since it was only for a short time, I knew there was a definite end. When I taught I felt energized because I participated in something I was passionate about, and once the class was over, that was that.

Fast forward two years. My current role at the church is Director of Volunteerism. My job is to connect potential volunteers to serving opportunities in the church that fit their God-given design. Within that, I regularly teach a spiritual gifts class. Looking back, I know teaching that one-time class was essential for me to confirm that ministering in this niche was God's call on my life. If I had remained in the pause mode during that season of my life, I wonder if I would have passed on the opportunity to teach the class that first time. I wonder if I would have missed out on a bit of spiritual formation that God had in mind for me.

And that's my point here. Even in transition, even in rest, even in status quo, God is engaged with us and wants us to be engaged with Him. When it feels like God is actively at work in everyone around us, but not in us, it's dangerous to conclude that God doesn't have anything for us. Like He put us in a spiritual cryogenic chamber and will thaw us out when He's ready for us.

Guess what? He's ready for us.

He is ready to use every opportunity to transform us into the people He wants us to be. And He will do it even when we are on the back line.

The Message Bible puts it this way:

> "You get us ready for life: You probe for our soft spots, You knock off our rough edges. And I'm feeling so fit, so safe: made right, kept right." (Psalm 7:9-10)

We sometimes feel like God is moving strongly and inviting us to action. In those times it is unmistakable that God is at work in us. But sometimes we find ourselves on the back line, when God's work in us is more subtle. In those times, God isn't putting our relationship on hold, but instead maybe just wants us to engage in a different way. Maybe it's a time of preparation. Maybe it's a time of redirection. Whatever it is, we will find it when we realize that being on the back line and being on a break are not the same thing.

Chapter 9
It's Not Impossible to Fly

Do you ever notice that when some memories come to mind you find yourself smiling as you think back to what took place? Sometimes you don't even know you're doing it. The smile just happens. Then there are those other memories, the embarrassing ones, or the ones where you blew it. When those come to mind it's more like a cringe that appears on your face. This chapter is about one of those. I subliminally cringe, not because there was a show-stopping blunder, but because we missed out on what could have been an amazing moment. You see, for a few minutes we forgot to believe that anything was possible.

One Tuesday night toward the end of a regular show, two actors were out front doing a scene while the rest of us were on the back line. We were watching, listening, engaged in the scene, doing just what we were supposed to be doing. Then Veronica, who was in the scene, declared that she could fly. It was a great moment. The new truth of the scene was that her character had the ability to fly. We all watched the rest of the scene play out, thoroughly enjoying what was unfolding, eventually getting to a place where we called "scene" and it ends.

Fast forward to after the show when we were downstairs in the green room debriefing the show. Liz looked at us who were on the back line during the scene and simply said, "Why didn't you guys make Veronica fly?" And we all looked at her and said, "Huh?" (Well, actually we just said that in our minds. But it's definitely what we were all thinking.) She continued, "Veronica needed to fly in that scene. You guys on the back line could have come out, lifted her up and made her fly. It would have been an incredible moment. The scene needed it. It would have been unforgettable!" Whoops...she was totally right.

Well, it was unforgettable, at least for me. That conversation, that scene and that missed moment, they're burned in my memory with regret about what *could* have been if we had been present in *possibility* instead of *reality*.

I think we were changed that night. We absolutely learned from that mistake and became improvisers who didn't miss out the next time. I felt this sense of hyperawareness for any chance to create the impossible with each other. It did eventually happen, and when it did, it was really cool. Yet for me, it was also bittersweet. Even as I write this, I still have a little bit of sadness about how Veronica didn't fly that night.

If I were to sum up what was missing that night, it would be *faith*. My friend Diana says that faith stands for **F**reely **A**llowing **I**t **T**o **H**appen. (Disclaimer: I'm usually not a fan of acronyms that attempt to define a word that already has a definition, but, hey, work with me…) I like the word "allowing" in that phrase. It makes me wonder how much we miss out on in our God-experience because we simply don't *allow* it to happen. We are held back by our fear, our doubt or our just being too grounded in reality as we were that night in the show. We forget that we are constantly presented with the chance to glimpse the impossible actually happen. And, better yet, to be a part of it!

This kind of faith doesn't come naturally for me. I tend to see a person or a situation for what it is, instead of seeing the potential of what could happen. But I am learning that believing something is possible is often a prerequisite to it actually happening. In Matthew 8:5-13 we hear about a Roman military commander telling Jesus about one of his employees, a servant, who was paralyzed. He wanted Jesus to heal him. He suggested that Jesus simply say the word, not even seeing the servant in person or touching him. Ultimately, Jesus did heal him that way *because* the commander believed it could happen. In fact, Jesus ends the encounter by affirming the man's great faith.

If it were me, I would have gone to Jesus and asked him to lessen my friend's pain or encourage him in this rough time or maybe give his doctors wisdom. Not that there's anything wrong with that, but when it comes to real faith, it would be the spiritual equivalent of standing on the back line and watching life unfold as it will, not expecting something incredible to actually happen.

Anyone who's read the Bible, specifically the gospels, notices that each author tells Jesus' story from his own perspective. Because of that, each of the books is a little different. For me, this isn't a reflection of inaccuracies in Jesus' biography but of personal perceptions of the writers. I think those events and teachings of Jesus that stood out to each gospel writer were what they often wrote about. And, I believe that the Holy Spirit prompted each of them to write what they wrote.

My point is that when we find a topic or truth from Jesus that is present in all four gospels, it must have been something that Jesus really drove home with His followers, something that they frequently dialogued about.

Faith, and what's possible because of it, is one of those topics. Here's what we find in each of the four gospels:

> In Matthew 17:20 Jesus said, "...for truly I say to you, if you have faith the size of a mustard seed, you will say to this mountain, 'Move from here to there,' and it will move; and nothing will be impossible to you."

> Mark 11:23 says, "Truly I say to you,

whoever says to this mountain, 'Be taken up and cast into the sea,' and does not doubt in his heart, but believes that what he says is going to happen, it will be granted him."

Luke 17:6 says, "And the Lord said, 'If you had faith like a mustard seed, you would say to this mulberry tree, 'Be uprooted and be planted in the sea;' and it would obey you.'"

John 14:12 says, "Truly, truly, I say to you, he who believes in Me, the works that I do, he will do also; and greater works than these he will do; because I go to the Father."

There are many more passages like these, but even when we take just these four we realize that Jesus taught about faith consistently. He taught about the kind of faith that makes the impossible possible. Can you imagine hearing Jesus say that with the smallest bit of faith, you could do wonders even greater than He did? From what I read in the Bible, that's exactly what He said.

As I mentioned a few minutes ago, I'm pretty far off from this kind of faith, so I find myself asking the question: How do I move in that direction? What baby steps might God be prompting in order to create faith in me – even a tiny mustard seed's worth?

From the verses I found in Matthew, Mark, Luke and John there's one thing stands out to me, at least in the first three. They tell me to say something. Say the words. Like, literally, pushing out these big belief words, even when they're backed by only a little faith.

"Mountain, move."

There's something about *verbalizing what could be*. I know there is power in words. I know that there is negative power in negative words. I see that in my relationships and even the inner conversation that loops in my brain. And there is also positive power in positive words. Words that are gentle, sincere and loving are life-giving to the person on the receiving end. When I speak uplifting, encouraging words to my daughters, they tend to live up to what I'm asking of them. We've all experienced the frustrating customer service situation that gets worse when we speak negatively, and somehow "magically" gets better when we speak kindly and respectfully.

All that to say, I think that faith starts with words. We should speak as if the best possible reality is actually true, in my relationships, in my situations, in my job, in my conflicts, in my marriage, and even in my head. This isn't the same thing as a "name it and claim it" mentality. It's simply a way to think and to speak where I keep my mind open to the possibility of something greater than my present reality. It's a way to live out the belief that more is possible.

My brother and I have a bit of a strained relationship lately. On the rare occasion that we talk on the phone, I go into the conversation waiting for the weird tension to begin. The negative words start to cycle in my head, and as the conversation goes pretty much how I predicted it would, I settle into accepting that our relationship will just always be less-than.

I got to see him a few weeks ago, and something kind of strange happened. I had decided beforehand that I was going to believe the best and say uplifting words that would help create a better reality for our relationship. He lives in Oregon, and our first day in the area we found out that he had been in jail overnight and was in a pretty serious situation that had turned his world upside down. As we talked and I made an effort to use uplifting words, I noticed a real difference in the way he and I were relating to each other. If you had been a fly on the wall you probably wouldn't have noticed anything real drastic, but for me I knew that I was getting more honesty, more sincerity and more vulnerability from him than I could ever remember. It was a pretty significant change from our pattern over the last 20 or so years.

I'm sure that some of this was simply due to the fact that he was in a rock-bottom kind of place emotionally, and it was just good to have some family to talk to. But looking back on it, I also think that God used his situation to soften my heart toward him, so that I would lose some of my cynicism and doubt. And because of that my words took on a hope that *more* was possible when it came to my brother and me. Now, don't get me wrong, I am still struggling to believe that our relationship can *flourish* but I think saying words like, "I love you," and "I know things will work out," and "Thank you for being honest with me" can be the beginning.

I'm not sure if the words create the belief or the belief creates the words. Maybe it's a little of both.

Jesus said that *belief* is the key, but He taught that the belief shows itself to be real through words. Faith is like this little bit of potential in your heart, that grows exponentially when it makes its way to your mouth. And, I guess, maybe, what Jesus was saying was that once that happens, you can fly.

Chapter 10
Make Each Other Look Good

One of the mandates of improvisation that has impacted me the most has been "Make Each Other Look Good." Wouldn't it be great to have an entourage of people around you whose whole job is to make you look good? At the office, they would wander the halls talking about how impressed they are with your work. At a dinner party they would laugh really loudly at your jokes and point out to everyone how you look like you've lost weight. Or when you are reading a bedtime story to your kids, your team would help you do funny voices and act out all the parts. (Better yet they would just do it for you, so you could relax and listen to the story with your child but still somehow get all the credit.)

On an improv stage you actually get this group of people. They are called your cast mates. The only difference is, that while they are busy making you look good, you are doing everything you can to do the same for them. Since improvisation is created by a team, the interplay among team members is of utmost importance. At the foundation of that interplay is the idea that it's *my* job to make everyone else look good. I don't need to focus on making myself look good because that is everyone else's job. Plus, I'm busy making them look good.

One of the reasons this idea made such an impression on me was that in the entertainment industry, be it acting, music, comedy, whatever, people typically need to position themselves in such a way as to get exposure and get noticed. You have to keep your best interests in mind and make decisions based on what's best for you.

Improvisation turns all that upside down. Great improvisers don't put themselves first and don't get preoccupied with being noticed. If I'm going to be a really strong improviser my drive must be to make everyone around me look good. It's about giving someone else the spotlight, giving them "gifts" and setting them up to succeed. When any player is self-focused, it hurts the scene. But, conversely, when a player becomes about the other players, he suddenly transforms into a strong and successful improviser.

One night at rehearsal, Liz showed us just how important this attribute is. To start the rehearsal she asked us to take a seat, so we all sat in the semi-circle of chairs, with Liz's chair opposite us. As we did, we noticed there was an empty chair. Normally we were all pretty good about arriving early or at least on time. But that night, Jane wasn't there yet. It was odd that she wasn't there, and it was odd that we would begin without her. And yet, here was our Director starting the rehearsal even though there was a glaring absence. I was just glad it wasn't me that was late!

What I soon learned, though, was something much bigger had happened. Liz looked at us and said, point blank, "I fired Jane today." (I've changed the name because Gabrielle would be mad if she new I used her real name. Doh!) We soon learned how Liz had been feeling for a while that Jane was missing some key ingredients that all improvisers need. One of the missing ingredients was to make everyone else look good. In her case, it wasn't a selfish trait as much as it was that she hadn't developed enough as an improviser for this to be a constant in her performance. In improvisation, failing to make each other look good can be a fatal flaw. Unfortunately for Jane, it cost her spot in the cast.

The funny thing is that while Jane's dismissal surprised us, we weren't surprised about why Liz made the decision she did. We had all felt it in our scenes with Jane. It was hard to trust that she would have your back or submit to what's best for the scene. In a weird way, by letting go of Jane, Liz herself was following the "Make Each Other Look Good" principle. Her job as Director was to do what was best for the whole cast, to make us, as a cast, look good. Eliminating a cast member who was hurting that outcome was a necessary action.

At it's core, the rule is about being in it for the good of other people and not for you. I think that's where it has become a spiritual principle for me. Ultimately, it's the very reason Jesus met us in our humanity, made Himself part of humanity. He died for our sins because we weren't "good enough" on our own. We needed Him, in essence, to make us look good. Now I realize that's a very superficial sounding way to put Christ's sacrifice, but by standing in our place He endowed us with perfect righteousness that we could never achieve on our own. This was the way of Christ, and the Bible again and again calls us to live like Jesus lived. What better way to do that than to work for the good of someone else, and not just me? If I were to think about what the best world would be, it would be one where every person's pursuit is to make someone else look good.

1 Corinthians 13:5 tells us that love is not self seeking. The words used in this verse mean that if you love you don't "strive after yourself." The implication is that if I truly love then I choose someone else's well-being over my own. It means that I go out of my way to give the other person the advantage. It's the overall idea of taking what is naturally an inward, self-focused view and turn it outward. It's to be about the other person.

Of course, there are a million ways we do this (or should I say, don't do this) but the one that I want to talk about has to do with credentials.

A few years ago I had a difficult and awkward conversation with someone I worked with at the church. He was my leader in one of the ministries I served in, and I was telling him that I was frustrated with how one aspect of our ministry was organized. I was trying to make the point that we would be able to do our ministry more effectively if we made this one change. And I told him that over the years I had seen this type of change work great, and even in seminary I had studied this particular model. I thought we should give it a try. I wanted to get him to catch the vision for how we could revitalize our ministry.

I wasn't trying to list my credentials. I really wasn't. But when I mentioned my background, immediately he got this look of intrigue on his face, and the resulting conversation went something like this:

"Wait, you've done this ministry before?"

"Yeah, at every church I've been a part of for the past 15 years or so."

"I had no idea."

"OK."

"What was your degree in at Fuller?"

"An MA in Theology."

"Wow...so what was your idea again?"

OK, so here's the deal. I suddenly had credibility because I now had credentials (or at least now he knew about them). And this is how it goes. We get reaction, attention and recognition when other people know what we bring to the table. So it makes total sense that we should present ourselves with our "best foot forward," so to speak. It's strategic, and if nothing else, easier. We can get what we want faster when we convince those around us that we know what we're talking about.

But here's the catch, when we do this we make it be about us. And spoiler alert: it's not about us! The New Living Bible says, "Don't be selfish; don't try to impress others. Be humble, thinking of others as better than yourselves." (Philippians 2:3) It comes so naturally to us to try to impress each other. It's a subtle game of one-upmanship, and the cycle perpetuates itself because when we do it, people respond, like the conversation I had with my leader. I wasn't getting anywhere but when I off-handedly mentioned something that impressed him, he was suddenly responsive to my idea.

And so we learn that if you want someone to

take you seriously you manage their view of you in a way that makes you look good. It's why our license plate holders bear the name of the prestigious schools we attended. It's why we post our degrees on our office walls. Now, hear my heart, I'm not saying there is anything wrong with a sense of accomplishment. I think God created us to feel satisfaction when we've worked hard for something. And let's be honest, I want my pediatrician's wall to showcase a degree from Stanford and not *Moe's Dockter School*.

Where it becomes a problem, though, is when impressing others becomes our objective. It's a problem when we look for ways to interject our accomplishments into a conversation, or when the game of one-upmanship becomes the norm. How can we listen to someone else, or appreciate them or learn from them when we are caught up in our own achievements? This mindset can evolve into destructive preoccupation with ourselves. And it's a far cry from the way of Christ.

If you keep reading in Philippians 2 you will come across what is probably a familiar passage:

"Though He was God, He did not think of

equality with God as something to cling to. Instead, He gave up His divine privileges; He took the humble position of a slave and was born as a human being. When He appeared in human form, He humbled himself in obedience to God and died a criminal's death on a cross." (Philippians 2:6-8)

He didn't rattle off His experience. He didn't prove that He should be in charge. He didn't aim to impress anyone. And because He abandoned His credentials, God the Father got to make Him look good, so to speak.

"Therefore, God elevated him to the place of highest honor and gave him the name above all other names..." (Philippians 2:9)

This is what is at the heart of making each other look good. It's quieting your need to self-advertise your own strengths and instead, putting your focus on those around you. It's bringing out the best in them, so that their strengths shine. And in that practice we will find that it is enough. That our sovereign and gracious God knows very well what we bring to the table and doesn't need help to create an opportunity for us to bring it.

Chapter 11
You Have to Know Before You Know

In improvisation, we make it a point to stay on our toes so we are fresh and ready for anything. This was a necessary objective considering our show changed nightly. I don't just mean it changed because the audience suggestions were different, and we never knew what the scene would become. I mean that the actual content of the show, the games we played, changed every single night.

To help you better visualize the show, let me take a minute to explain "games." Games were the different structures for the scenes in the show. Everything was called a game. In a given show we would run about 10 to 12 games. For example, one game we often played was Take That Back (or TTB as we used to call it. Improvisers like to shorten things. An economy of words so to speak. So we took it from three syllables to...um...three syllables. Wait a minute...doh!). In TTB we would start a scene with an audience suggestion. We'd ask, "What is a location that could fit on this stage?" And they'd yell, "Bathroom!" or, "Train station!" (albeit a small train station) or, "Coffee shop." So we'd start the scene. But off to the side was a cast member who wasn't in the scene holding a bell like the type you'd find at a service counter. Anytime throughout the scene the bell-ringer would hit the bell, and whoever last spoke would have to change what they just said to something else. The bell ringer could ring it as many times in a row as she wanted and the players in the scene had to accept whatever was the last thing said as the new reality. So it might go like this:

> Player 1: We better get packed up. The feds will be here any minute.

> Player 2: I hear a siren! (ding) I hear footsteps! (ding) I hear voices in my head!

Player 1: I know, Joel. Your meds are running low. We'll stop by a pharmacy once we get out of here. (ding) We'll go to your house and get some more. (ding) We'll run to Mexico. I hear you can get that stuff over the counter there.

That would be considered a game of TTB. Really, any scene mechanism is called a game. And one thing that kept us sharp was that we typically wouldn't know what games we would be playing in the show or what order they would be in until we got there that night. Once in a while, if we were lucky, we would get an e-mail that afternoon with the running order. (Abbreviated "RO" There, see, we saved two syllables on that one!) But typically there was little advance warning. We'd see the RO then 45 minutes later, we'd be on stage performing it.

This was just par for the course, but sometimes this process would cause me to have a slight panic attack. Many of the games I loved. Some of the games I was afraid of. I loved the games where you could just have fun and be ridiculous. You could make up characters and scenarios and everyone had a good time. I was afraid of the games where I was required to perform based on something real where it was fairly likely that the audience knew more about the subject than I did. Or, even if they didn't, they would know that I didn't know.

Once we took an audience suggestion, we would have to incorporate it into the parameters of whatever game we were playing. Such as…

Tell a story in the style of author Booth Tarkington…huh?

Or, create a scene that takes place in the country of Svalbard…where?

Perform a monologue as if you were a quantum chromodynamicist…I'm sorry, a what?

On the outside I put on a happy face and just went with it. On the inside I was like "What are you talking about?!? I've never heard of Svalbard!! It sounds like a boating term to me!" When we had to ask for an author, I'd silently be pleading "Please someone yell out Dr. Seuss! I know that guy!"

But here's the deal, whether you know something or not is irrelevant in improvisation. Liz would constantly tell us, "You have to know before you know." In other words, you have to find this place in your brain where confidence overrides knowledge. You must become confident in knowing something that you don't actually know.

If you actually knew what a quantum chromodynamicist was you would say things like, "Consistent with non-abelian gauge theory, the quarks and gluons show asymptotic freedom at high energies." (That's right...I know how to use Wikipedia.)

But when you are improvising, you would say things like, "Consistent with our bliggety bloggety theory, we have determined that there was no molecular goo or doo hickies at all on the thingamajig."

And because it is improvisation, both of these statements are right! When you refer to doo hickies in your scene, doo hickies actually exist. Of course they exist! You're the quantum chromodynamicist after all, right? (Never question the guy with the word "quantum" in his title. It sounds like he might be able to shrink you.)

In a nutshell, knowledge is not the most important thing. Making your knowledge the reality, even when you don't really know from personal experience, is the most important thing.

I drive a minivan. It's sad. It's not the minivan's fault, but I have a little bit of resentment that it's what I drive. I just never pictured myself driving a minivan. Maybe a classy SUV or even a cute four-door sedan, but a minivan? No. When I drove off the lot after buying it, there was a little part of my soul that died...the cool part to be specific. (sigh).

I will say on behalf of the minivan that it's been a great vehicle. Recently though, the "check engine" light came on. That's always alarming. Especially since I know nothing about cars, but doubly so because Chris also knows nothing about cars. His idea of mechanical prowess is to Google Precision Auto down the road, then give me the number so I can call and make myself an appointment.

So that's what I did. I dropped it off, they took it for a few hours and magically when I got it back the "check engine" light was off and I was out 376 bucks. When the light was on I didn't notice anything different about how it drove. No weird sounds or anything. Now that I had it back it sounded just the same. I have no idea if anything had really changed. For all I know they could have just disconnected the wire that turns on the light behind the words "check engine."

But strangely, I have confidence that they in fact did not just cut the light, but that they repaired the actual problem. I have a lot of confidence that this is the case, although I have nothing to base that confidence on other than the fact that I trust those guys behind the counter.

I know even when I don't know.

Is it unrealistic for God to expect me to have the same confidence and trust in Him that I have in the Precision Auto guys?

God wants me to know before I know. He asks me to trust Him because of who He says He is. I can choose to know Him regardless of my experience, or lack thereof, because I can believe what He says about Himself.

Take any one of God's traits: His power, His love, His faithfulness or His forgiveness. The truth is while we can experience bits of God's character, we can't fully know the extent of who He is until we see Him face to face. I'm not saying that to diminish anyone's personal experiences with God. We certainly can have very real interactions with Him. But even the most poignant experiences with God are just a glimpse of what is to come. They are the tip of the iceberg, the trailer for the movie, the tiny percentage of our brain that we actually use.

I say that not to minimize the now but to emphasize that the vastness of God is beyond our wildest imaginations. And what I know of God through my limited experience is enough when it's added to what I "know" about God simply because I am confident that He is who He says He is, regardless of my personal and experiential knowledge of Him.

Think about it this way. There are two different kinds of knowledge. There's cognitive knowledge and experiential knowledge. Cognitive knowledge, for example, is how even if you've never *been* to Paris, you still know that it exists. Experiential, on the other hand, would be overlooking the city from the top of the Eiffel Tower. (The one in Vegas, by the way, does not count.) On any given topic, a person could have one or both of these kinds of knowledge.

So, when it comes to God's love, for example, Ephesians 3:17b-19 says,

> "...and I pray that you, being rooted and established in love, may have power, together with all the Lord's people, to *grasp* how wide and long and high and deep is the love of Christ, and to *know* this love that surpasses knowledge—that you may be filled to the measure of all the fullness of God." (Emphasis mine.)

The word "grasp" in this passage means to lay hold of something with your mind, to comprehend it or, to mentally own it. This is head knowledge. It's what I'm calling the "know-before-you-know" kind of knowledge. It's not necessarily based on your experience, but you "know" it nonetheless. In addition, Paul wants his readers to "know this love that surpasses knowledge." He's talking here about experiential knowledge, about experiencing God's love at a depth that allows you to *know* it because you have *felt* it in a very real way.

So in the full context of the verse, knowing happens in your mind, grasping and comprehending, that God loves you *and* actually experiencing that love because you believed in it. It's knowledge that has come full circle.

But I think often the cycle begins with a choice to believe in God's love. It's that first step of faith that says, "I will grab onto this truth about God whether I see it in action or not." And in so doing, the potential to experience it truly unfolds.

Now don't get me wrong, of course God can flood us with His love however and whenever He chooses. He works through what we think (and in spite of it). He lives through our experiences (and in spite of them). He can communicate His love for us any way He wants, head first or heart first. I'm merely suggesting that when there is, in fact, a lack of personal experience it doesn't mean that our knowledge of Him is likewise limited. His character is unchanging, and as we learn about Him we come to know Him.

And the best part of all is that even if it were possible to fill our brains to capacity with knowledge of God, it would still only be a blurry glimpse of the reality.

"For now we see only a reflection as in a mirror; then we shall see face to face. Now I know in part; then I shall know fully, even as I am fully known." (1 Corinthians 13:12)

On stage we did our best to act as if our performance came from a place of knowledge, from our actual, personal experience. But many times that just wasn't the case. In those instances it was enough to act like we really knew. When it comes to knowing God, there is a lot we are missing this side of heaven. But it doesn't mean we can't live like we really know. For now, it must be enough to know before we know.

Chapter 12
Good Improvisation Takes Rehearsal

So by now you get that improvisation is about making stuff up on the spot. But if you've ever watched improvisation done well, it can be hard to believe that it really is made up right then. Once in a while after a show we would hear what I think was the greatest compliment, "You guys don't really just make that up do you? I mean, it must be planned!"

It's like a really good cook having someone ask her where she got the recipe for the incredible dish she just served. And the cook says there was no recipe. She just made it up!

So when we were asked if there was secretly a script, we'd say, "No, really. We just made it up."

To be honest, sometimes I was even amazed at how well a scene would turn out, because with improvisation, you just never know. You don't know what line someone will say. You don't know what suggestions the audience will offer. You don't even know when the scene is going to be over. But you just go with it, and you believe that it will work. And to be part of it when it did work, was an incredible thing.

One of the places where people had the most difficulty believing the show wasn't scripted was during the musical numbers. We always had at least one musical section of our shows where we'd sing a song that we were making up as we went along. Our musical director was an amazing, talented musician named Don. Don would sit at the piano during the whole show and play along. He would underscore, accompany or sometimes just make sound effects that would add to the scene. So, of course, he was making it up as he went along, too.

When everything went right, there were times that the piece came together so organically that we would literally sing the same thing at the same time, and Don would be playing right along with us. When this happened, it was kind of surreal and euphoric.

How is it possible to be that connected and have our instincts so in sync? These were the moments that an onlooker would find it hard to believe that it wasn't scripted. When we assured them that it was truly improvised I often felt like they didn't fully believe us, but again, I took it as a compliment.

Now, I don't mean to come off like I'm tooting my own horn. Like, "Hey, I'm so great that people assumed the material had been written for me. I'm a genius of improvisation!" The truth is that I often felt like the weakest, least experienced player of the group. It's not even about that. It wasn't about any one of us. The connectedness was like this whole other entity among all of us. Liz called it "Group Mind." Whatever it was, it took a lot of work for us to hone in on it and trust it. But when we did, the results were pretty powerful.

And where we did the work of honing in was in rehearsal. That's right, rehearsal. "Wait," you say, "why do you have to rehearse if it's all just made up? You aren't really even making it up, are you? Is this actually scripted?" Then I say, "No, listen. Haven't you been paying attention to this chapter? Why am I even telling you all this? Please try to focus." Let me explain.

The rehearsals were all about teaching us to connect and to trust each other. Sure, we would go over the logistics of how to play a certain game that we might be doing in the show. But once that business was out of the way, it was time to hone in on the Group Mind. Rehearsal was the place where you took big, crazy risks and weren't afraid to fail. It was where Liz pushed us to let go of our inhibitions and just go for it. We had to commit to the scene and to each other even when we didn't know what would happen or how to solve the dilemmas that came up in the scene. And the truth is, sometimes we didn't solve them, and the scene was just a big flop. These not-so-compelling scenes also happened in the shows once in a while, but we don't want to talk about that. Just forget I mentioned it.

As we did these exercises in rehearsal though, regardless of how they worked out, what always resulted was that each person in the group felt supported, embraced and appreciated by every other person. As Liz taught us how to be better improvisers, such as how to play the games better and how to enhance the scenes more, what she was really teaching us was how to be a team that valued and respected each other. A team that was so inherently connected to one another that our scenes felt planned. That's why we had rehearsal.

In our spiritual lives, rehearsal is when you invest in your connection with God. It's the stuff you do together with Him that builds trust, intimacy and like-mindedness. If I were to carry out the metaphor, our actions and how we live out our lives would be the show, and the one-on-one time with me and God would be the rehearsals.

I had a youth leader once who talked about those parts of a relationship with God that were "behind closed doors." She said that we get to have a relationship with God that's *personal*. It's between Him and me. We have a connection that's unique, because I am unique. What I have with God is unique to me and God. And what you have with God is unique to you and God. That's how relationships work.

I often focus a lot on the results part of my relationship with God. How am I doing at using my gifts? Do other people think that I am a loving person? Am I living out the fruit of the Spirit? These are important questions for sure. But I think I skip the rehearsals sometimes. I neglect the part of my spiritual journey that's about me and God connecting.

Connecting with God is a weird concept if you think about it. The all-knowing, all-powerful Creator wants to connect with me on a personal level! What's *that* supposed to look like? I find solace in the fact that there is not a formula, and it's not a one-size-fits-all solution. Sure, there are disciplines or practices that we can build into that relationship, but the moments of true connection often come in surprising ways.

Have you ever had one of those experiences where in the middle of an ordinary, "non-spiritual" situation you've had a completely extraordinary and very spiritual moment with God? This happens for me in the car a lot. Sometimes it's that you sense His presence strongly, and other times you have a very clear impression about something He wants you to know or do.

But what connection looks like is maybe not the question we should be asking. Instead we might ask, "Why does God want to connect with me? What happens in me that can only happen when I connect with God?"

In Ephesians 1:17-19 Paul says,

"I keep asking that the God of our Lord Jesus Christ, the glorious Father, may give you the Spirit of wisdom and revelation, *so that you may know Him better*. I pray also that the eyes of your heart may be enlightened in order that you may know the *hope* to which He has called you, the riches of His *glorious inheritance* in the saints, and His incomparably great *power* for us who believe..." (Emphasis mine.)

There is so much packed into that verse! It's one of those passages in the Bible that makes me think, "Even if I just lived out this *one* passage, I would be doing pretty good spiritually."

That you may know Him better, and in so doing:

Know the hope.

Know the inheritance.

Know His power.

Hope...

As we connect with God we begin to experience hope. We have hope in how our story ends. This hope is what empowers us to press on even when the life we are presently living falls so short of what we expected. Hope that truly resides in God does not diminish in the face of disappointment with the here and now.

Inheritance...

As for "His glorious inheritance in the saints," this is an interesting phrase. When I've read this verse in the past, I thought it referred to what we will inherit as children of God. Ephesians, earlier in the chapter, talks about being adopted into God's family, so it makes sense to think in terms of our inheritance. The riches of who God is are handed down to us as His children. That is certainly true and probably part of what this verse is talking about.

But these three little words "in the saints" are what stood out to me more recently when I read it. If the verse was strictly talking about what we will inherit from God, you would think it would read "for the saints" instead. "In the saints," on the other hand, gives the impression that *we* are the inheritance that God is being given. God's inheritance is found in us!

So if this is true, let me first just say what we are all thinking, God is getting the short end of the stick on this deal! Now, with that out of the way, I find it fascinating that as the Holy Spirit opens up our hearts and our understanding to know God, the outcome is that He gets us. As we live a life in pursuit of knowing God, we are building a relationship with God where in the end, we get each other. I get Him because He gave Himself to me fully in Christ. He gets me, because I am His inheritance. In the end, we get each other.

Power...

And then there is that power. The power that we experience from our connection with God is the same power that raised Jesus. The remainder of the passage says, "...and His incomparably great power for us who believe. That power is the same as the mighty strength He exerted when He raised Christ from the dead and seated Him at his right hand in the heavenly realms."

This power made Christ come back to life, and this same power is what makes us come alive. When we seek to know God better, His power brings life to our bones and breath to our lungs. It makes us really alive!

So when it comes to our connection with God, there is so much at stake. Because He created us He is able to keep creating us and transforming us. He is the only One that can bring our potential to fruition.

This kind of transformation involves hope, inheritance and power. God wants to connect with me and wants me to connect with Him. That's exactly why I was created in the first place! In the end that's what it's all about. It's hope for what will be. It's knowing that we get each other. And it's laying hold of power that proved itself in the resurrection. So we move toward knowing Him, all the while recognizing that we've only just begun our relationships with Him...we're still in the rehearsal.

Chapter 13
Don't Give Each Other Notes

I love giving advice…even when no one asks me for it. I think it's because I have opinions about everything, and I'm a talker. I like to talk, and I have opinions. Which means I tell everyone my opinion which means I give a lot of advice. Did I mention that it's not always asked for?

I guess my friends take it in stride. I tend to have more friends younger than me than older, and I sometimes wonder if it's because I know deep down that I can bestow my years of wisdom on them. Or at least I can try. Hey, they're the ones who told me about the problem with their mother-in-law…how can I help it if a genius solution suddenly comes to my mind? So, anyway I like to give advice. Did you get that?

Although I had trained as an improviser for several years before I joined the cast in Las Vegas, in many ways when I started in Scripltess I had a sort of crash course in improvisation. You know how they say that the more you know, the more you know that you don't know? It often seems the more advanced in a given topic you become, the more you realize just how much there is yet to learn. That's how I felt my first few months in the show, like I was just getting my feet wet with the whole craft.

I joined the cast with the belief that I must have proved myself in the audition, and that someone out there in the darkened theater saw some talent. In these kinds of auditions you're often on a brightly lit stage. And even though you can't see past the third row, the powers-that-be (a.k.a. those judging the audition) find it necessary to sit way in the back. You can't see their faces or read their expressions. So there you are hoping and praying that they think you've got what it takes, but since you can't see them at all you just have no idea. Until that big cane comes out of nowhere and drags you off the stage by your neck. So goes the audition.

Needless to say, in an audition where hundreds of people come from all over the country and you are lucky enough to be one of the few that gets a "yes," there is a sense of prideful competence. And, for me, what came with it was a nagging question of how long would it be before someone discovered that I didn't know what the heck I was doing?! I kept thinking, "I fooled them in the audition. (Yay!) But now I have to perform on a Las Vegas stage in a show where there is no script! (Insert expletive here.)"

So began my dual personality. On the outside I was the picture of self-assuredness, while on the inside I was like a hungry sponge hoping to soak in everything I never learned in an attempt to pass myself off as someone worthy of the "yes" that I had already been given.

It's probably not lost on you that there is a strong spiritual parallel right there, but that's not where I'm going with this. Try not to jump ahead.

There were a myriad of truths about improv that I learned in those first few months, but one that really stuck out to me was the rule, "Don't Give Each Other Notes." Basically, you may not, under any circumstances, give a cast mate negative feedback or direction about their performance. You can't do it before a show. You can't do it after a show. You can't do it during a show. You can't do it through an anonymous note taped to their locker in the green room. (Trust me on that one.) There can be no suggestions or correction given from one cast member to another. Do you know what another word for "suggestions" or "corrections" is? That's right...advice. No giving advice! It's frowned upon. Translation: it won't be tolerated. Translation: it's a cardinal sin of improvisation. One of Liz's favorite sayings was, "Shut your pie hole." (Said with as much love as possible, of course.) That saying applied to this rule in particular.

The "Don't Give Each Other Notes" rule offered security, like those rules that are for your own good. What made it possible to be vulnerable, take risks and explore ideas on stage together was knowing that a peer would never give you notes. The Director would give you notes. That was her job. But you knew that she was doing it objectively and with the big picture in mind. She was doing it to make you better, both as a team and as an individual player.

So we all heeded this rule. And if, in the rare instance one of us had a momentary lapse and gave another a note, you would always hear someone else in the cast say, "Hey, no giving notes!" That was usually me, because it was a sly way to get away with giving advice.

On the whole the "Don't Give Each Other Notes" thing was relatively easy to put into practice. It was, after all, a very black and white rule about what could and could not be said to one another. You just didn't do it, plain and simple. Later, much later, I learned that this rule was really only a surface layer of a deeper, more important, more foundational tenet of the craft.

And that is, don't judge each other. Now, I realize that the phrase "don't judge each other" is not pithy or sexy or intriguing. If anything, it might have just elicited a sigh and eye roll from some of you out there. But if you'll indulge me for a minute, I hope to share with you what I've learned lately about my tendency to judge in my own relationships. For now, let's get back to improvisation...

In a scene, only when you don't judge can you say yes. Only when you don't judge can you accept a gift. Only when you don't judge can you make the impossible possible. Only when you don't judge are you able to make each other look good. Only when you don't judge can you lose the filter.

I hope you are seeing a pattern here. Only when you don't judge can *any* meaningful improvisation be done. It is at the heart of everything. Period.

In the middle of an improvised scene, judging is basically a series of thoughts, criticisms, questions or evaluations that occur in the improviser's head.

Why did they say that?

That wasn't a good idea!

I can't believe they made that choice.

That was low-hanging fruit...they always go there.

I wish someone else had come off the back line to be in this scene with me.

There they go again just trying to be funny.

That's a boring character.

You get the idea. It's the voice in your head that won't stop evaluating. These patterns are detrimental to the scene even when you are just thinking them. Because the truth is that somehow negative thoughts undermine your responses and begin to build a wall between you and the other actor in the scene with you.

It took a long time for our cast to stop judging each other. Every time the temptation to judge what someone else did or said in a scene, we had to mentally dismiss it. Then we had to embrace their contribution with no reservation. And as we did that more and more, something interesting started to happen. The more we intentionally suppressed our negative opinions, the less and less frequent they became. Until eventually, our minds were trained to not even go there. The thoughts simply had no place in our relationships on stage. Of course, when we got lazy or lacked discipline, the old patterns would emerge, but we tried to nip it in the bud by temporarily working harder to eliminate them, until it was second nature again to not judge each other.

Looking back it's easy for me to see why the deeper truth, "Don't Judge," took so much longer for me to learn. When you don't give notes, you simply control what you say. Worst case scenario, you have to bite your tongue. But when you don't judge, you have to control what you think, which is not so simple. The saying "bite your brain" never really took off for a reason.

So here's the weird thing I discovered about judging in real life...

Most of the time, when I have judgmental thoughts about someone else, it's about preferences or personal style. I don't mean clothing style here, but let's face it, some stuff people wear is just tacky! That's right...I said it! I don't consider that judging. That's just stating a fact. What I mean by personal style is an individual's set of preferences or way of going about things that differs from my own.

I tend to do things a certain way because I think it makes the most sense. For example, I pay the bills all at once every few weeks instead of paying each one as soon as I get it. It's not right or wrong. It's just what I think works the best. Or, with the glove compartment, for example. I know that some people keep theirs filled with just the basics: manual, registration, insurance. I, on the other hand, consider the glove compartment to be the convenience store of the vehicle. It includes napkins, extra phone chargers, lotion, gum, pens, Band-aids and spare change. I like feeling prepared, but it's just a preference. It's my way, my style, my approach.

And even though I know this decision about how I pay bills or organize my glove compartment is totally subjective, and lots of very smart, successful people don't do it my way, I somehow start to think that my way is the best way. I admit that there are other ways it can be done, but deep down I really think my way is better. I mean, I wouldn't be doing it that way if I didn't think it was the best way, right? And inevitably, without even realizing it sometimes, I start to look down on other people when I learn that they do this thing a totally different way.

Here's a relational example for me. My sister-in-law Reese has a very different parenting style than I do. Any of you who parent or even just have kids in your life know that most parenting styles fall somewhere in the middle of the spectrum between the extremes. But for some reason, Reese and I usually end up on opposite sides of the spectrum. And just to keep it fair in my description I won't give away which one is me and which one is her, but here's some of our parenting differences.

One of us had her baby sleeping in the crib from day one. The other one did co-sleeping (where you all sleep in the same bed) for the first couple of years.

One of us breastfed exclusively for a few years. The other one used formula.

One of us got an epidural and happily stayed in the hospital until the doctor told her to go home. The other one went natural and even did a home birth, never going to the hospital at all.

One of us used cloth diapers. The other one of us used disposable.

Now I realize not knowing which one is me might bug you, but try to get over that and see my point. Even in those little examples, many of you probably had a strong reaction to one side or the other. And that strong reaction almost immediately turns into judgment. "No way! I can't believe she would give birth at home! Is that even safe?" Or, "I can't believe she left that poor little baby all alone in the crib at night. What if she didn't hear the baby crying? How selfish is that!"

So here's the deal. This is all style stuff. There's no absolute right or wrong way to parent. You do what you think is best for you and your child. Yet, it's so easy for us to confuse the right way to do something with what just happens to be our way. And this mentality translates into so many other areas of life beyond raising kids. It slips into our marriages, our work ethic, the way we spend our money, our communication styles even the way we decorate our houses.

On a spiritual level, these style preferences can get in the way of us experiencing what Jesus came to bring in all our relationships: peace, acceptance, support and encouragement. Paul talks about it this way in Colossians:

> "Make allowance for each other's faults, and forgive anyone who offends you. Remember, the Lord forgave you, so you must forgive others. Above all, clothe yourselves with love, which binds us all together in perfect harmony. And let the peace that comes from Christ rule in your

hearts. For as members of one body you are called to live in peace. And always be thankful." (Colossians 3:13-15)

How can we put our energy toward building a strong, unified connection to each other, when we're too busy judging each other over inconsequential lifestyle choices?

And trust me when I say that I'm talking to myself just as much as I'm talking to you. For me, this is something I have to constantly remember. It was so easy for me to get into a "my-way-is-best" mindset that snap judgments had become my norm. When I noticed this happening in me, I started looking closer at what it really means to not judge. And I realized that there are a couple of different categories when it comes to judging people.

Category 1: Helpful, constructive and necessary thought processes that enable me to make wise choices in my life. An example of this would be if I see someone run a red light, and I think, "That was a dumb move." This falls into the category of necessary thought processes that help me not make the same mistake I see someone else make. This is also judging, but it's the good kind. (Kind of like how there's good fat and bad fat. Mmmm...bacon.)

Category 2: Unnecessary judgment based on preference and style. I see someone driving a red car, and I think, "That is the ugliest color for that car! Don't they know that red attracts the cops? They are an idiot for driving a red car." Then it falls into the category of thoughts that say my way is the best. (Did I mention that my minivan is dark blue? Very subtle. Just blends in to the flow of traffic. I'm just saying.) This kind of thought process quickly evolves into a dangerous habit of judging anytime, anywhere without even noticing that I'm doing it.

If I was trying to figure out whether my thoughts were Category 1 or Category 2, I would ask myself this question:

WHO CARES?

As usual, I've blown your mind! Oh, I didn't? Well, hear me out on this one, anyway.

I would ask myself, "Who cares?" Who *really* cares? That guy's driving a car that I don't like. Who cares? That lady chews her gum like a cow. Who cares? That church sings cheesy songs. Who cares? That guy smells. Who cares? That parent lets their kid stay up until 10:00 on a school night. Who cares? That couple went out to a dinner that was way too expensive. Who cares?

If I could put a "who cares?" on the end of my thought, then I knew it was an unhealthy pattern. I mean, in the grand scheme of life, in the big picture, in the spirit of let's-not-make-a-mountain-out-of-a-mole-hill...who really cares if that person doesn't do things the way I think they should be done???

So here's my advice to you. (Hey, don't act so shocked! I told you I like to give advice.) My advice is to find the line for yourself between Category 1 and Category 2. And then, to the best of your ability, stick to Category 1. Category 2 seems harmless. It's often just thoughts after all. But know this; it will never be possible to "clothe yourself with love" while your thoughts still reside in Category 2.

Chapter 14
Stop Talking When the Lights Go Out

A few years ago I was one of the narrators for our church's Christmas Eve production. We had six services planned and, as you can imagine, the very first one was followed by a group huddle to discuss how it went. We had Music Guy, Tech Guy, Stage Girl, Drama Girl, and Bible Guy (also known as our Senior Pastor), virtually every leader responsible for the production.

We huddled up and proceeded to discuss, evaluate, rearrange, alter and eliminate. We all wanted it to be the very best service it could be. This was our last chance to put the final touches on what we'd given our hearts and souls to for the better part of the past four months.

There was one bit of narration that none of us felt great about. I was tasked to rewrite that bit, memorize it for the following night and deliver it in such a way that it flowed seamlessly into Bible Guy's message. So that's what I did. I added a few lines to the original ending, and everyone felt like that would work just fine.

Fast forward to the next night...I was focused. My partner was focused. The audience was eating out of our hands. We were like a well-oiled machine with each piece working flawlessly to deliver what was sure to be a moving moment that melted everyone's hearts in preparation for the message.

One problem. One tiny, itsy-bitsy problem. Tech Guy forgot to write the new cue lines in his notes.

I'm on a roll. I'm gearing up for the newly added and quite moving (if I do say so myself) set of lines. I deliver the original lines. I get to the original ending. I take a breath to launch myself into what is sure to bring people to Jesus then and there. And I notice a strange thing happen. A subtle dimming of the lights begins to take place. No wait, it's more than subtle. No wait, they're fading. Noooooooo! Blackout.

Hmph.

This all happened a while after my Las Vegas improv career had ended. But I was suddenly brought back to that kind of split-second moment where a decision must be made...Now!

And in about five-eighths of a second I had an internal conversation with myself that went something like this:

I should just keep talking.

No, you can't keep talking! The lights went out.

I know, but you haven't heard the life-changing stuff I was about to say.

It doesn't matter! No lights, no lines.

But they really need to hear this.

Maybe next service.

But I had it all planned out! It was meant to be. God-ordained even.

Now you're going a little far.

How will Bible Guy get through to them? It's my job to soften them up!

Isn't that what the Holy Spirit is for?

Yeah, that's what I mean. It's Him...and me.

I'm sorry, but it's too late.

What do you mean it's too late?

When the lights go out, the scene is over. That's the rule.

These people don't know that rule.

In improvisation, this rule I'm talking about has everything to do with a cast member I haven't told you about yet. It's the Stage Manager. Contrary to what the title might suggest, the Stage Manager is neither a manager nor located anywhere near the stage. It's different, I guess, than in other acting-related venues. But for some reason, in our show the Stage Manager was the one who ran the actual performance from a booth way in the back of the theater.

As you know by now, we (the actors) don't know where the scene is going, what will happen next or when it will end. We just keep talking until the lights go out. The Stage Manager is the one who makes that call. And when that happens the scene is over. I know…it's a clever and subtle signal to those of us onstage that we should stop talking now. Hard to miss the pitch blackness that instantaneously descends on you.

And that's how it goes. Or should I say, that's how it ends.

It works because we trust the Stage Manager. Those of us in the scene are biased and involved. We don't have any sort of "big picture" perspective on what's going on, so we wholeheartedly accept and respect the Stage Manager's authority to end the scene. I'm not saying we always agreed with the Stage Manager's call, but we complied with it because that was her role. Our role was to keep going until the lights went out.

When the lights go out there's nothing left to say because the scene is over. Even if you were about to deliver the most clever line in all of improvisational history, you don't. Because guess what? That's right, the scene is over.

I'd like to tell you that this training, this rule, that had been ingrained into my thinking from my improv years took over during the five-eighths of a second conversation I was having with myself during what I now refer to as the "premature Christmas fade out."

But it didn't.

I deliver the original lines. The lights go out. I just keep going....

Then awkwardly, ever so awkwardly, the lights come back up and before me is a sea of confused faces. What just happened? Was it supposed to go that way? Do we clap now? WWJD?

And that's when it really sank in: "When the lights go out, the scene is over." Amen.

I have a friend who has been struggling for a while now with a romantic relationship that ended. It wasn't her decision to end it, although in retrospect she knows it was the right thing. But she can't get this guy out of her mind. When she goes to the places where they used to hang out, she secretly hopes she'll see him. When she talks to their mutual friends a little bit of her hangs on to the hope that they will mention him and that maybe he's been asking about her. She knows it's over, but she can't seem to let it go completely.

I met a guy a while ago who was a recent transplant to the Bay Area, where I live. He moved here because he got laid off in his previous position and consequently couldn't make his rent payments each month. He came back here to live with his parents for a while and to get back on his feet emotionally and financially. Every time I talk to him he mentions that he still hasn't made very many friends and how he'll never find a job as good as the one he had. He's still trying to find a way to get back there, and I don't fault him for that, I just wonder if his mindset is getting in the way of him moving on.

In both these situations, my friends are trying to cope with loss. Yuck. We hate that word. Loss. It stinks.

We lost our luggage once on our way back from a vacation in Spain. I mean really lost. We didn't get it back a few days later or even weeks later. We never got it back! It's like it vanished into thin air, but I can't help but wonder if some one in Spain might be wearing my stuff as we speak. But the joke's on them because I was very pregnant at the time so good luck fitting in my pale blue pajamas with a 52" waistband. Ha!

Real loss though? Real loss is unfair. It's unexpected. It's usually more serious than pale blue pajamas. It can throw us off balance so severely that we forget which way is up.

I think one of the most blatant biblical examples of loss is the life of Joseph. Again and again he encountered loss. And over his lifetime we see him accept that loss and continue to trust God. His life went something like this:

Grew up with favor and freedom in his large family.

Then…

LOST freedom when his brothers sold him into slavery because they were jealous of the favor he had received.

Then…

Transferred eventually to Potiphar's house where "the Lord was with Joseph and he prospered…the Lord gave him success in everything he did…and he found favor in [Potiphar's] eyes and…he put him in charge of his household." (Genesis 39:2-20)

Then…

LOST favor and position when Potiphar's wife falsely accused Joseph and he ends up in prison.

Then…

Rose to position even in prison because "the Lord was with Joseph and gave him success in whatever he did" (Genesis 39:23) and interpreted dreams of the baker and the cupbearer.

Then...

LOST opportunity for release when the cupbearer forgot about Joseph for two full years.

Then...

Interpreted Pharaoh's dream, ultimately leading to a position in Egypt second only to Pharaoh himself.

When a relationship, a job, money, status, a position, a dream or (fill in the blank) ends on someone else's terms, it's almost impossible not to feel like we've been left in the dark in a scene that we thought was going somewhere. The lights went out, and there was nothing we could do about it.

Joseph's life was filled with heart-wrenching loss that would leave most of us shaking our fists at God and saying, "Why me?" Joseph probably had those moments too, but at the end of the day, he walked the path that had been laid out for him. He had seasons of brilliantly lit success that were eclipsed by darkness many times over. Yet in the middle of this senseless loss, he trusted in God.

Sometimes it's God Himself that cut the lights. But in an effort not to over-spiritualize let me tell you what I'm not saying:

> I'm not saying that when stuff gets taken away, it was God that did it.

> I'm not saying that on a whim God might snuff out a relationship in which you have invested.

> I'm not saying that when humans take from you more than they should, and you feel a sense of loss, it's because God wanted it that way.

In fact, I'm not trying to say anything about the *why* of loss. I'm saying that when we do experience an end that we weren't ready for, God might expect something from us in the way we react.

I think He might expect us to not keep going that way.

Again, indulge me a few clarifications about what I'm not saying:

I'm not saying that we should just shut off our emotions and get over it.

I'm not saying that God expects an instantaneous release on our part.

I'm not saying that when you lose someone you should put on a brave face.

All I'm saying is this…

God intervenes. God wants what's best for us. God is willing to take something away if that loss will help us be more like Him. Or He's willing to use the loss that He didn't cause to draw us close to Himself. I think, in that way, God is a great user of resources. He can and will use whatever is at His disposal for our good.

He cuts the lights. Or sometimes He lets someone else do it.

When the lights have gone out a on piece of my life, I've found that when I follow suit and let it go, it enables and even prepares me to be ready for a new thing to begin. Or sometimes I just need to sit in the dark for a while. And that's OK too.

It's not so much about how, when or why the lights go out. It's really all about my trust in the Manager. (Unlike Tech Guy, God doesn't make mistakes. He is the definition of trustworthy.) Trust is about submitting when the answer is "No." It's not about hoping that maybe there is enough dim light that I can struggle to keep going down a path that I'm not ready to abandon. No, it's about hoping in a God who sees and who loves. It's about His constancy regardless of the lights.

At the end of Joseph's life he makes his brothers promise that when the Lord ultimately delivers them from Egypt, they will take Joseph's bones with them to freedom. Even in the face of his death which is his final loss, he trusts in a God that is bigger. And he looks forward with anticipation to what's next.

Chapter 15
Be in the Moment

Living in Vegas and getting the opportunity to act in a live show there impacted me in a significant and memorable way. I learned so much about life, comedy and faith. I want to share about one last "rule" that really impacted me. In many ways it is at the heart of all improvisation. It has to do with moments.

We all have these moments in time that stick in our brain and become an intrinsic part of who we are. My most memorable wedding moment: I was standing next to Chris, and the sun was streaming through the stained glass that made up one whole wall of the little church. It washed over us, seeming to soak us in its warmth, as we listened to a beautiful worship song.

My most memorable "funny-things-my-daughter-Quinn-says" moment: She saw my friend nursing, and after learning that the baby was drinking milk, she asked, "Does the other side have juice?"

My most memorable theme park moment: I was in fourth grade when my mom and my aunt Brenda took my cousin Ani and me to Six Flags Magic Mountain. It was an extremely hot day, and Ani kept complaining about how hot she was. We were in line for Roaring Rapids when the heat got the best of her, and she flat out fainted right there! I remember thinking, "Wow, I can't believe she fainted. Do we still get to go on the ride?" and that was my last thought before I fainted, right on top of her. (The answer is No, by the way. You don't still get to go on the ride. You do get wheeled to first aid where they put a cold ice pack on your head. Then your mom tells you that you have to go home.)

My most memorable new-to-Vegas moment: I was sitting at a red light waiting to turn left, and I saw about 37 Elvises traipsing down the sidewalk like it was an everyday occurrence. (I know. Some of you are thinking that this *does* sound like an everyday occurrence in Vegas, but trust me it's not!) That's when it hit me that I actually lived in Las Vegas.

It's fascinating to me which moments stick out in my memory. I find it interesting that a moment, one little speck of time, can burn itself into my experience and stay there for years, even decades. I don't know how my brain determines which moments are remembered. But I'm really glad these moments are captured, because one thing about moments is that when they're over, they're over. This is particularly evident in improvisation.

For example, in every Scriptless show we would create new characters as part of a scene. And just as we were getting to know those characters, POOF! The scene would be over and the character would be gone. I know it sounds silly but sometimes we missed those characters. Does that ever happen for you? Like when you get to the end of a fictional book, and you realize that you have to say goodbye to these people that have felt real to you. Everything is this way in improvisation. Sometimes when a scene ended we would joke and say, "It's sad, we'll never know what happened to that couple."

> You create a scenario, but you only get to
> live in it for a few moments, then POOF!

You make up a funny, creative musical number, then POOF!

You dialogue with your scene partner, building an interesting relationship between the two of you, then POOF!

We'll never get to see those moments again.

Quinn likes me to make up songs to sing to her. I've actually gotten to be pretty good at it. I suppose I got a lot of practice in the show. In fact I sing made-up songs to my kids more than I sing real songs that everyone knows. Most parents sing "Old MacDonald." We sing about Renaldo and his flying monkeys. (And trust me, it is not easy to come up with an impromptu rhyme for Renaldo. He tends to play a lot of "Where's Waldo?") Inevitably, when I get to the end of a particularly funny or sweet one she says, "Sing it again!" Then, with a little bit of teasing, I say, "Sorry, Honey, you can't ever hear that song again." It sounds sad, but actually it's become our little joke. I tell her that when you make songs up you have to enjoy them while you're hearing them, because you'll never be able to recreate the song exactly as it was. She just laughs and tells me to sing a new one.

"Be In the Moment" was a phrase my cast mates and I heard from Liz on a regular basis. In improvisation, "being in the moment" means that you are present mentally, emotionally and physically in whatever is happening right then. Being *present* means that you are in the *now*. You aren't thinking ahead or planning what might come next. You aren't dwelling on what happened five seconds ago. You are fully engaged and fully available to the *now* of the scene.

Being in the moment is necessary in improvisation. You can't listen or accept gifts or heighten very well without being fully present. But these are not the only reasons to stay in the moment. Being present in a moment is the only way you can fully enjoy that moment.

Many improvisers can't get enough of improvisation. It becomes an obsession. They sign up for classes as a hobby. Then within a few months, they improvise at any chance they get, form a troupe, watch improvisation whenever possible and start hanging out with a bunch of other improvisers. They're hooked! And there's no turning back.

Improvisation has this power to draw people in, because the moments you create together are like nothing else. They are unpredictable. They are moving. They are often hilarious. They are organic. They come about because the improvisers are willing to take huge risks again and again. Improvisers put themselves out on that stage with no backup plan. Sometimes they fall and sometimes they fly. And the reason it grabs you, both as performer and onlooker, is that you won't know which one it is until the very moment it happens. Improvisation compels you to be fully invested in every second, knowing that you'll never experience that exact moment again.

What would it be to embrace this concept in every aspect of our lives? Psalm 103:15-17 says:

"Our days on earth are like grass;
like wildflowers, we bloom and die.
The wind blows, and we are gone,
as though we had never been here.
But the love of the Lord remains forever
with those who fear Him."

One of the reasons the Psalms are so powerful is that they speak candidly to the realities of life. In the grand timeline of humanity, the life we live is a little flash. Of course it doesn't feel that way on the days where you get up at 6 a.m., and you don't see your pillow again until past 11 p.m. at night. But deep down we know that time flies by quickly. I vividly remember the sun streaming through that stained glass, but it astounds me that it was 12 years ago. Every time I see my parents, they have a little more gray hair than the last time I saw them. (And, let's be honest, I see my own gray hair making an unwelcome appearance.) We've lived in the Bay Area for almost three years now. Where did the time go?

As the years go by I find myself with this gnawing fear in my gut. I'm afraid that I'll look back on the last two or five or even 20 years and find that I haven't made much of a difference. Or worse, that I haven't transformed into being more like Christ. That I am just the same person I was before, with nothing tangible to show for my moments.

I hate that fear.

I think that fear and I have a sort of healthy rivalry, though. It triggers a desire in me to live toward my fullest potential. It's the desire to impact my friends with God's love. So I focus more energy into my relationships. It's the longing to experience real transformation. So I pursue Jesus more wholeheartedly, more sincerely. And it's the determination to make a lasting mark on this world. So I write a book. (Books last, right? Dang it. I knew I should have made it hardback!)

This past summer during a family vacation, I got a visual about life's brevity that has stuck with me. Quinn and I signed up for a morning horse ride through the wooded hills in Southern Oregon. Our guide, Jack, was a mix between an old Harley biker guy and a cowboy. He was full of stories and details about what we were seeing on our ride. As we meandered through the trees I kept noticing these blue dots. Several of the trees had mug-sized blue circles painted on their trunks. I said to Jack, "What's the deal with the blue dots?" He told me that those trees were marked to be cut down. I was hit with a wave of sadness and said, "Wow, that's a shame. It's so beautiful out here with all the trees!" Jack continued,

> "Yeah, well, they've got to thin out the trees sometimes. Those will get cut down at some point. But I've been riding this trail for years, and none of them have been

cut down yet. They just stay there with their blue dots, waiting. It will happen eventually, but no one knows when."

I kept thinking about those trees, and I realized that I have a blue dot too. My time is limited. All of our's is. Unlike the trees though, we have the ability to do more than just sit and wait. So I will choose to invest in the moments. I will discover and then do what I was created to do. And through it all I will remember that God's love doesn't have a blue dot. "But the love of the Lord remains forever with those who fear him." (Psalm 103:17) We are compelled to live fully engaged in the now, because that's what it means to really live.

We have certainly covered a wide range of improvisation rules, but the truth is that good improvisation all comes down to this one principle of being fully present in the now. All the other rules hinge on an improviser's ability to "Be in the Moment."

When I consider the spiritual life, and everything we've talked about so far, it seems to me that much of our spiritual journey also hinges on the ability to "Be in the Moment," to be fully present with God in the now. It's being connected to God. It's responding to His presence in our lives. It's listening to His words. It's believing in His character. In a nutshell, it's relationship.

God taught me about Himself through the unlikely outlet of a Las Vegas show. And He can use the most unlikely things in your own life to do the same for you. I hope that as you consider the tenets of improvisation and apply them to your own spiritual journey, you are encouraged to live a life that is Scriptless.

About the Author

Andrea Coli brings out the best in people by communicating biblical truth with humor and insight that will inspire any audience. She has a deep desire to help others understand their innate uniqueness, and capitalize on their God-given strengths and talents. Her greatest thrill is seeing truth discovered and lives changed because of it.

Having worked full-time in both ministry and business, Andrea relates to people no matter where they are on their spiritual journey. In addition, her background as an improviser on the Las Vegas Strip makes her quick on her toes and full of surprises. Her seminary education provides a solid foundation for sound Biblical teaching, and her sense of humor makes it all a lot of fun.

When it comes to retreats and women's ministry events, Andrea loves to teach on topics and passages that fit the direction of each unique group. Crafting a fresh message is what inspires her and allows God to use her in unique ways with audiences. To hear messages she has done for other groups, recordings are available upon request.

Andrea also specializes in staff development

training. She offers hands-on personality workshops that enhance team cooperation and is available to work with staff or ministry teams.

Andrea received her MA in Theology from Fuller Theological Seminary and resides in the San Francisco Bay Area with her husband Chris and their two daughters.

For speaking engagement inquiries:
925.858.2989
scriptless.book@gmail.com

74342621R00100

Made in the USA
San Bernardino, CA
15 April 2018